But I Never

Thought He'd Die

But I Never Thought He'd Die

PRACTICAL HELP FOR WIDOWS

by

Miriam Baker Nye

THE WESTMINSTER PRESS
Philadelphia

Book Design by Dorothy Alden Smith

FIRST EDITION

Published by The Westminster Press®
Philadelphia, Pennsylvania

PRINTED IN THE UNITED STATES OF AMERICA

9 8 7 6 5 4 3 2 1

Library of Congress Cataloging in Publication Data

Nye, Miriam Baker, 1918–
But I never thought he'd die.

Includes bibliographical references.
1. Widows—United States. I. Title.
HQ1058.5.U5N9 301.42'86 78-9644
ISBN 0-664-24208-1

To the memory of Carl E. Baker, 1916–1970

CONTENTS

FOREWORD

A suggestion offered in my homemakers' column some years ago brought an unexpected response from readers. I had pointed out that a widow who is faced with holding a sale of farm machinery and livestock needs guidance on the subject. I had just groped my way through such an experience. I thought the state university extension service should publish such a pamphlet. Within a short time, many of my readers urged me to attempt preparation of a sale guide myself, based on what I had learned the hard way.

I might have tried to write such a guide for farm widows if I had not become involved in a project of broader scope. Through correspondence and numerous informal conversations I learned that widows wanted help in thinking through many diverse problems they were encountering. They had emotional needs, worries about guiding children without fathers, concern over employment and residence choices, desire to invest time and energy in something "worthwhile," and doubts about making anything good of a role they had never expected to fill—the widow's role.

Those same concerns had suddenly become vital to me on a storm-swept twelfth of May. A freak accident, caused by gusty wind and rain-slick pavement, instantly took my husband's life. We had set out to do some business in the city, and had traveled less than five miles from home when the wind caught us.

Carl received multiple head injuries when the door beside him swung open and the car overturned. Held by my safety belt, I received the merest scratches on my nose and knees. I was "lucky," some people said. How did they know what it meant to be happily married one minute and a fifty-one-year-old widow the next?

Looking back, I can see that certain understandings could have helped me immeasurably in the early weeks and months of widowhood. There was so much that bewildered, frustrated, and wounded me. If only I had had in my hands a practical, trustworthy "guide to widowhood"!

In her letter to me after work on this book commenced, a widow of one year wrote, "I need help *right now* in deciding whether to stay in my large home or make a change of residence." Another woman concluded her letter with the wistful words, "Do you find yourself wondering sometimes if you're really sane or not?—I hope so, for I sure do."

Many popular "widow" books found on the shelves of stores or libraries dwell either upon the initial period of grief, confusion, and change, or upon how a widow can attract eligible men. The theme of this book is not "How to Succeed as a Widow," nor "How to Be a Merry Widow," nor "How to Endure Widowhood." What is offered is a guide for fact-facing, understanding feelings (yours and others'), identifying and carrying out developmental tasks, and setting new goals.

If you can say, "Why, that is one of my problems, too, but I haven't really admitted it or dealt with it" or "There's an idea I can use or can profitably reflect upon," the effort of getting the book together will seem worthwhile. There is also a strong hope of contributing to the understanding of caring persons around you—your friends, your family, your pastor, and others who would be supportive in widowhood.

ACKNOWLEDGMENTS

The varied contributions of many women and men who gave friendship, understanding, and wise counsel to me during widowhood or during the writing of this book cannot be listed individually. Where illustrations from their experiences have been used, fictitious names and initials have been assigned.

Professor Louise C. Johnson, Director of Social Work at the University of South Dakota, guided me through independent reading in professional studies of widowhood. She also served as "sounding board" critic as the sections and chapters of the book were written and presented for consideration.

John Nye, to whom I was married in 1973, gave steadfast encouragement throughout the period of intensive study and writing.

Dr. Robert Jewett, Department of Religion, Morningside College, evaluated much of the manuscript as it progressed into later stages. Others who read and commented helpfully on selected chapters were Attorney Glenn C. Metcalf; Economist Dr. Donald A. Watson, University of Oregon; my journalist son, Kent Baker; and Mrs. Frances Vargason, a single parent.

1

Since It Happened to You

When you promised to be your husband's wife until "death us do part," you really didn't accept the possibility of being left behind, did you? Most of us didn't. No wonder we felt abandoned, afraid, shaky, and singled out for suffering when it happened.

It is natural to assume at first that no one can understand how devastating your loss is. To find out that some others *do* understand, that others care, that others are capable of sharing your grief, is perhaps the most positive factor in facing bereavement.

One recent widow spoke of being strengthened by her conviction that God was sharing her sorrow. She also discovered that reading of the experience of a woman who, like herself, had been widowed at a time when many more years of married life were anticipated, brought comfort and encouragement to a faltering spirit.

A friend of mine who is a middle-aged homemaker was left to rear a small daughter years ago when her first husband died. She had no widowed friends her own age. But she read in the newspapers of the many young women being widowed during World War II. She sensed silent comradeship with them, understanding how they felt.

When an accident killed my husband, who had shared life with me for twenty-nine years, I was especially touched by the understanding messages written to me by women who had lost their husbands. Some letters were written by women I knew personally. Many others were from women who read my weekly column. Their expressions of sympathy were not flowery, but honest and real. They knew what I was going through and what lay before me. They urged me to continue my writing.

I am aware that commonly practiced etiquette does not require bereaved persons to write thank-you notes to those who have sent cards—only to those who have given flowers or memorial donations and those who have helped with food or tasks. But I made sure that a personal note went to every widow who had taken the trouble to write to me. It took months to get them all written and mailed. I could never forget how much it meant to hear from others who could say truthfully, "I know how hard it is" or "You will be strengthened according to your need."

Remembering my own shock, bewilderment, and utter weariness, I appreciate in retrospect the sensitivity of the close friend who watched for the "right time" to give me a book she had purchased for me and my sons—Gladys Kooiman's *When Death Takes a Father.*[1] I do not think I would have been ready to read it in the very first weeks of bereavement.

But I am glad that book's message reached me when it did —in the second month of widowhood. I read it eagerly. It gave me an opportunity to discover that another woman had faced loss and risen to life's new challenges.

Widow statistics may never have impressed you until "it happened." Now, the knowledge that you are among many can be strengthening, once you realize your position and open yourself to communication.

You may have read that at any given time, one out of three women in the United States lives alone, whether she likes it or not. Some live alone by choice. But many live alone because the spouse who once shared life has left earthly existence.

Recent figures state that the United States has more than eleven million widows and widowers, more than one million of them under fifty years of age.

In pioneer times of the past century, many women died young. Men often outlived two or three wives. But the era in which we are living seems to produce more and more widows. The chances that an American wife will become a widow are now so great that such an eventuality should be considered by every thoughtful married woman.

Yet fear of death and bereavement prevent all but a few from making preparation for widowhood. Some women have a superstitious fear that any such planning might hurry the death or that planning might indicate that the death is desired. Some wives are simply not used to planning. Others want to avoid the pain of looking ahead.

A man whose wife was ill with cancer several years confided that as they shared the knowledge of her coming death, he could face the prospect of events up to and including the funeral. But he could not bring himself to look past that time. He could not think of life as a man alone. What he expressed is quite common to married persons whose mates are terminally ill.

The circumstances in which death comes will be quite varied. You probably lost your husband (1) as the result of lengthy illness and suffering; (2) because of a known and threatening condition, lived with for a period of years, for example, high blood pressure or heart trouble; (3) through a sudden attack or sickness, without advance warning; or (4) in an accident. A smaller number are bereaved through suicide or homicide.

When you talk with others who have been bereaved, opinions may be volunteered as to which kind of death is "harder" for the survivor. Those who have lost mates suddenly admit their deep shock and confusion, but tend to feel sympathy for people they know who have sat for months by beds of pain, suffering along with their spouses.

Likewise, those who have been informed that death was on the way admit their anguish and exhaustion, but are quick to sympathize with bereaved friends, who complacently thought married life would continue to old age. "How tragic," they say, "to be brought to grief in one terrible, shattering moment!"

When we have not permitted ourselves to think about possible loss of the mate, until death forces us to do so, we stand in acute need of help. We may draw rather feebly upon vague memories of the ways in which widows we know have met problems. But we will derive more vital strength and support from contacts with understanding persons who are able to listen and relate to us.

Crushed by loss and weighed down by unexpected responsibilities, we may well be desperate for the kind of assurance that women and men who have risen from emotional depths themselves can offer. Those who communicate effectively their own struggles, their recognition of the aspects of grief, their personal development during a period of transition, can enable us and encourage us in our necessary mourning. They can help us also in our assimilation of bereavement as a major life experience with potential for growth.

Face-to-face contacts are limited for all of us. That is why you can be heartened to discover that identifying with people you meet on the pages of a book adds to your courage and vision. Inspired by others, you can become more open to healing and to beckoning opportunity. You can change from widow into woman.

2

Facing Up to Your Loss

How many times have you been told: "You will get over your loss if you just don't dwell on it. . . . You will *never* really get over your sorrow. . . . If you get it off your mind, and think about something else, you'll be all right again. . . . No matter what you do, you'll keep remembering how your life used to be. . . . The best thing you can do is keep busy"? Are these the well-meant but contradictory promises and predictions of your relatives and friends?

Have some of your associates declared that there isn't any hope of genuine relief from the depressed feelings brought about by the loss of your husband? Have others assured you that if you promptly become superactive in church and community affairs, or if you get a job, you will almost immediately "get over it"?

The bereaved soon discover that most members of our present-day society do not understand the importance of "grief work." If you have not already felt the stigma of giving in to grief, you probably will. To let such feelings show is generally regarded as weakness. Failing to have self-control is thought inconsiderate; it makes others uncomfortable.

In one of her talks, Mary Brite, of Omaha, declared that widowhood is like being cut down the middle with a razor blade, then told, "Now heal, and function!"[2] An unnamed Pennsylvania widow wrote to *THEOS Newsletter* that she felt "so empty and unhappy." "I am involved," she wrote, "in various things, but I really do not have my whole heart in them. . . . Sometimes I want to scream and scream. . . . This is the hardest test of my life and I seem to be continually struggling. At times I question my faith."[3]

Yet most people praise the new widow who is "taking it well." They commend the one who is "carrying on as usual." They give high social marks to the survivor who hides emotions and keeps companions from feeling awkward or uneasy.

The harm done by those who try to force the bereaved to pretend cheerfulness is surely as great as that done by those who gloomily state that one *can't* work through grief to the rebuilding of life.

Through conferences, workshops, and the study of books on dying, today's nurses, doctors, morticians, clergy, and nursing-home employees are learning to listen to and talk with terminally ill patients and their families. But who understands and counsels those who have been left behind? You may not have found even one person in whom you can truly confide, one who knows how to be supportive throughout the duration of grief work.

The chances are that most of the people around you have never studied professional books or articles to learn the normal phases of grief. It may be that neither you nor your friends recognize the denial and disorganization that ordinarily precede reorganization following bereavement. Relatives, neighbors, even doctors and ministers may attempt to shut off your mourning prematurely. Their glib maxims, prescriptions, and devotional booklets may satisfy the givers but do little for you.

Not understanding the need for thorough grief work, most people do not realize the amount of time that may be needed for working through. Only a few cultural groups now set definite time periods for grief.

The Orthodox Jewish way has concentrated intense mourning in the first seven days. Some of the steps are: sons or other relatives keeping vigil while the body is in the house; burial within twenty-four hours unless death occurs after sunset on Friday; all close relatives wearing ritually cut garments during seven days of "sitting shiva"; mourners returning from the cemetery to sit on low stools, unwashed, unshaven, unspeaking, and waited upon; visiting from those who discuss the deceased, looking over photo albums, and recalling incidents in the life that has ended. The mourning continues with further ritual for thirty days and still other traditions carried out for eleven months.

Both Church of Scotland (Presbyterian) and Roman Catholic communities formerly had strict rules of mourning. Many of these customs were brought to America by the colonists. But in the present-day United States, mourning practices seem to have been largely diluted or abandoned.

According to William A. Lessa, "Deritualization has set in so markedly in American funeral customs that younger generations know of the practices of a few decades ago only through hearsay. . . . Church funerals continue, but processionals and recessionals are very simple. . . . With the increased recourse to cremation, the ritualistic aspects of funerals have received less and less emphasis.

". . . Black clothing is no longer prescribed, and the black armband has virtually disappeared, as have black-bordered handkerchiefs, black-bordered stationery, crepe veils, and mourning jewelry. . . . Doorbells are no longer hung with crepe streamers or flowers. . . . Messages of condolence and acknowledgements of sympathy are brief.

"Excessive manifestation of grief is regarded as a bid for sympathy and therefore in poor taste. . . . The death notices inserted in newspapers are restrained. The period of mourning has been shortened and sometimes eliminated altogether except for simple observances by very close relatives who . . . define the period of mourning by their own preferences in the matter."[4]

The purpose of many of the traditional mourning customs was to give the bereaved person a distinctive appearance, which would motivate others to respect the mourner's situation. Another reason for the customs was to make provision for withdrawal from social activity over a prescribed period of time. When the calendar indicated that enough months had passed, a woman might begin to wear lavender instead of all black. Later she would make the change to white garments, and finally to the "milestone red dress" in some cultures.

When you and I became widows, there was no such schedule for grief and no such outward indication of our progress through it. Our changing society has an amazing mixture of mourning customs and rejection of customs. Some religions deny the existence of death. Some teach reincarnation. Many people question traditional funeral and burial practices, often opting for shorter and simpler plans. Abbreviated ritual, private burial, or leaving one's body to a medical school have become more common. One can't tell how long a woman has been a widow by her dress. Yet the bereaved person's need for an adequate grief process is as strong as in any previous generation.

How Grief Work Is Prevented or Delayed

Unless you realize the importance of grief work, you may delay it, resist it, neglect it, or permit others to block it. You may thrust grief experience aside, with a brave display of being "very strong." Or your family and friends—with good intentions—may keep changing the subject, trying to steer you away from anything "too upsetting."

One act of my own grief work was especially slow to be accomplished. It could have been done much sooner, and afforded me marked relief. I was troubled by my imperfect memory of the accident that took my husband's life.

An investigating trooper, who happened to have been a guest in our home a year or so before, came to me at the hospital. He asked a few routine questions regarding the accident. I could not reconstruct it very well, despite the fact that I was scarcely injured and never lost consciousness.

It seemed to me that the car had rolled over once, perhaps twice. I had had the feeling of being rudderless in space. Exactly how the car overturned, yet landed right side up, headed in the opposite direction from which we had been going, puzzled me.

I heard afterward that there were reports of a strong wind noticed by a nearby farm family, and a gust that swept another car from U.S. 20 a few miles farther east, at about the same time as our accident. I struggled to remember what happened in the seconds just after we seemed to be pushed off the wet paving by a giant, invisible force.

When I thought about this during sleepless nights, I felt it might help me to go out to where the accident had taken place and walk in the car's path. (The marks still showed in roadside vegetation.) Perhaps I could understand how the car left the road, how the door on the driver's side came unlatched, how the fatal head injury was received, though Carl's safety belt was fastened.

When I first expressed a desire to go to the scene and walk around a few minutes, my sons shook their heads determinedly. They had both gone to the local repair shop to which the wreck had been towed. They insisted that I must not put myself through the strain of seeing the car. They felt just as negative about my going to inspect the accident scene.

Later on, when I was living alone, I still wanted to go to the scene of the accident. But I knew it would upset any friends who might chance to drive by and see me there alone. I could not think of the right one to ask to accompany me on this brief but important journey. Some were busy. Others would have thought me morbid.

Almost a year had passed when my sister and her husband came from Oregon for a visit. Don, who had not been back since Carl's death, was an interested listener as I reviewed a little of what had been experienced the previous May. All at once it occurred to me that he might be the very one to help me inspect the accident scene.

A clear thinker and well informed, he was able to visualize and verbalize what had taken place. Having himself survived a crash years before, he understood how badly I needed to make my way mentally through the happening, how I wanted to put the whole thing to rest. He went with me to the scene, and patiently talked through the tragic happening in its various aspects.

Accomplishing this part of "making the past history" had been postponed unnecessarily. But fortunately, when this part of my grief work was finally done, it was done thoroughly. It brought a great measure of relief.

With the very best intentions, caring individuals who want to help may prevent mourning. One widow's close relatives took all of the deceased husband's clothing and personal possessions out of the house while she was absent. They thought they had done a kindness. It did not occur to them that they had destroyed a natural opportunity for the widow to review her marriage, to think of her husband's significant acts, now and then having a good, private cry as she sorted his effects.

The demands of your job, or the well-nigh frenzied attention given to it, may result in postponement of grief work. Students of widowhood have noted that widows with employment outside the home generally adjust more quickly to their loss of a mate. But throwing yourself tirelessly into a paying job or volunteer work is no guarantee of emotional healing. As a matter of fact, illness may overtake the widow who pushes to *keep busy.*

You may think you are earning exemption from mourning by exhausting yourself daily. But when the job's hours and responsibilities shut out reminiscing, review of your marriage relationship, writing thoughtful thanks, disposing of clothes and belongings, household rearrangement, or planning for the future, the effect upon you is one of increasing inner pressure.

Janice Q.'s well-meaning friend almost succeeded in blocking the mourning process with an effort to "busy" her at the earliest possible moment. She telephoned Janice, a widow of just one week, urging the bereaved woman to accompany her to a meeting about a local conflict.

Janice and her late husband had been leaders in trying to improve communication between the town council and the local taxpayers. Surely she would want to get right back to where the action was!

When Janice refused the offer of a ride, pleading fatigue and indisposition, the caller became insistent! "You must get out right away. . . . It will be good for you. You need to be busy."

Actually, a widow usually *is* busy. Even when a couple's business affairs have been well managed, there are numerous details to attend to in the early weeks and months of widowhood. During characteristic inertia, resulting from a widow's temporary lack of energy, even the simpler business chores seem overwhelming.

"I needed time to mend," recalled Helen Hayes, the actress. "I needed quiet time, apart time. Grief is a very feeling thing. If I had had a chance to sit still and indulge in grief, I think it would have made my recovery much quicker, shorter."[5]

Grief work may be resisted by trying to avoid seeing or hearing anything that reminds you of the loss. Some widows go at once to stay with a married son or daughter, unwilling to face the pain of seeing the husband's clothes or tools or favorite magazines lying around the house.

I recall such an instance in which a widow would not return to her own home for many weeks after the death. Her adult children were severely tried. They pretended that they wanted their mother to remain with them as long as she wished, while confessing to friends that they didn't know how they could ever help her feel secure enough to take up residence alone.

Not only did the mother plead that she "just couldn't go back there," she sat around, sad-eyed and apathetic, no longer interested in her grandchildren's progress, her friends' visits, or her daughter's obvious need for household help.

Her sons had to take care of their mother's business concerns and see that her house was checked daily. They felt she could be attending to her own affairs with far more satisfactory outcome. If only she would accept her loss and her new role before their patience wore thin!

Grief is sometimes resisted because the mate who died forbade tears. Dolores M.'s husband told her, during terminal illness, that she must keep smiling for his sake. After the death she managed to appear cheerful in her sales work and a few social activities.

The length and intensity of Dolores' repressed grief was indicated when she confessed that "it has taken years since Keith's death left a knot in my stomach the size of a grapefruit to diminish it to the size of a peanut." A voice inside Dolores saying "if only Keith were here" remained disturbingly insistent. It forced her to earn extra money for a vacation trip. She did not feel justified in enjoying anything she and Keith as a couple could not afford.

Ignoring grief and neglecting grief work have become common in our society. We tend to specify shorter and shorter funerals, some of them private, or "only graveside." Offers of assistance with meals are refused by some, who declare they want no appearance of "feasting." By the refusal our neighbors are prevented from acting out their sympathy. And we deprive ourselves of the opportunity for reminiscing around the table, initiating needed grief work.

Resistance to, or abbreviation of, mourning brings serious consequences. Physical symptoms often noted are loss of weight, rheumatism, asthma, chest pains, various ulcers, indigestion, skin irritation, and headaches. Commonest of all is difficulty in sleeping. Neurotic behavior may develop. Various forms of dependency may result.

Those who do not make their way *through* the denial of loss may keep on indefinitely hearing the deceased's voice or footsteps, talking to his photo, imagining him present, refusing to act without first asking the dead husband's opinion. This kind of fantasy is now recognized as more common than had been thought previously. For a while it can be a comfort to those who had no forewarning of loss. But it is potentially a form of dependency.

A widow I know related how she received comfort from talking with her deceased husband, but eventually gained self-confidence: "Sometimes I talked aloud to Eddie and to God as I drove somewhere in the car alone, or as I lay in bed at night. For a good many months—maybe a year—I did this frequently. I had a friendly chat with both Eddie and God, rather than prayer by the usual definition.

"I took cues from God and Eddie. Accepting guidance—yesses, noes, and not yets—was easier than it had ever been for me. More quietness and privacy than at any other period of my life made it possible for me to confide and to listen.

"I gradually ceased addressing conversation to my husband, Eddie. Acceptance of his death, and growing confidence in myself as a single person, freed me of the need to 'consult' Eddie. I continued to pray to and talk with God."

Assuming the identity or the characteristics of the one who has died is another grief phenomenon seen occasionally. Commenting upon her experience of taking on her husband's identity, the psychotherapist Alice Ginott told a news reporter: "To bury a man takes only a short time. To give him up to the past takes much longer. I would not let him die.

"Unconsciously I transformed myself into the man I had lost. I spoke his language and performed his deeds. I gave up my work to continue his. I wrote in his style and gave his speeches, and even made him coauthor of my work. I held onto my dead husband by burying the self that was me."

Eventually recognizing her dilemma, Mrs. Ginott concluded: "I found I could either become a different kind of person, and separate myself emotionally from my dead husband, or remain stuck in that disintegrated state. I finally discovered that I could live without him. You can wail and regress for the rest of your life, or make a life for yourself."[6]

Alcohol or drug dependency is the plight of some widows who have been unable to "mourn well." Overeating is another form of dependency in widowhood. Becoming abnormally dependent upon persons—family members, the doctor, the pastor, or the attorney—may result when mourning is retarded.

Suicide, the most extreme consequence of all, occurs as a bereavement reaction among those who have found no capacity for accepting and assimilating sorrow. A widowed person who fears that a suicidal tendency is developing should turn at once to a doctor able to give help or ready to refer the patient to a doctor with suitable training and experience.

Grief Stages in Retrospect

Looking back, I can see now the stages of my own grief: (1) shock and numbness, (2) disorganization, and (3) reorganization. Knowing the expected phases and recognizing where one is in the process can be helpful in terms of both reassurance and motivation toward life's new patterning.

To be at first unable to believe what has happened is entirely normal, both for those who suffered loss after lengthy illness of a spouse and for those whose loss came without warning. To act as if you hardly know how different life will be is part of the initial numbness. You may manage to hold up very well through the days of planning and carrying out funeral rites. You can appear calm partly because you do not yet feel all the pain of separation as you will be able to feel it later.

Thank God for the blessing of numbness! It prevents us from sensing the full extent of bereavement at the outset. By degrees we accept and integrate the loss of a beloved person into our life experience.

Nurses in the emergency room where my husband and I were taken following our accident told my parents they did not see how I kept from breaking down. At my request, they brought a telephone. I called each of my sons at their respective colleges, telling them of their father's death. I urged that each should find a friend to accompany him on the journey home, and cautioned them to drive with extreme care.

From my hospital bed I set in motion arrangements for a private burial (relatives attending), followed by a memorial service in our church. This was according to a plan Carl and I had several times discussed, pledging ourselves to carry out the plan for the other if necessary. But my mind had not fully taken in the fact of death while I rested twenty-four hours at our doctor's insistence.

Mindful of my weekly deadline, I jotted down the words of the first stanza of "O God, Our Help in Ages Past" and sent them to be printed with the lines "In Memoriam—Friend Husband, born November 13, 1916, died May 12, 1970," as the sum total of that week's "From the Kitchen Window" column. (Carl had been referred to as F. H. [Friend Husband] from the time I began to write in 1953.)

Hospital visits from family and close friends began to make the death real to me. Awareness increased when sons Kent and Dale took me home to the farm the next day. The first thing I saw was the Ford pickup truck, still standing where Carl had parked it before we started for the city in the rain. The dejected look of Pepper, our Collie dog waiting nearby, accentuated our loss.

The following morning several relatives gathered downstairs while I lay sleeping in the "master bedroom," now suddenly become the "widow's room." Awakening, I had a poignant recollection of Carl as a "morning person," full of vigor after he had slept. Never again would he be there to greet me, to challenge me with the work and play of a new day. Great sobs shook me. Numbness was wearing off. The pain of separation was asserting itself.

As a widow in the period of disorganization you may do absurd and foolish things. You may overlook mealtime, ignore traffic laws, make impulsive purchases beyond your means, forget dates and hours of meetings you have always attended faithfully. You may abruptly change some parts of your setting and life-style without careful consideration of long-range plans.

Though such actions are normal for the phase of disorganization, they may be quite upsetting to you and to those around you. Be glad if a few friends have the patience and understanding to stay in close touch when you are so unpredictable, even irrational at times.

During my own widowhood disorganization I did not know to what extent I should try to carry on my husband's farm operation. At first I attempted to think as he thought, decide as he would have decided, act as he would have acted. But questions were arising for which there were no precedents in his twenty-year conduct of the farm business.

When people offered advice, I often wavered. After the sale of our machinery and tools, I unwittingly continued to pay insurance premiums on them. Although I had a full crib of corn on hand, I was persuaded to buy corn for feeding out the turkey flocks that had been started. It did not even occur to me then that there would be only the early flocks, no late flocks to eat the cribbed corn.

After sealing the corn (something Carl had never had reason to do), I worried over whether I had done the right thing. Months later, I lay awake nights deciding exactly when that corn should be sold. Some knowledge had been gained. But business acumen could not develop readily when my whole life was in flux.

Eventually I realized that I was not fitted for and did not want to substitute for my husband in the farm operator's role.

I might be able to learn to fill a landlord role satisfactorily. It was important for me to affirm my own abilities, different from Carl's.

The need to find a basis for making business judgments was only one of many widowhood needs I had during the period of disorganization. Personal priorities, my relationship with my sons, my friendships, my church participation, my living arrangements were all out of joint in some ways. Proceeding to a time of reorganization was vital if a satisfying life as a woman-on-my-own was to be built.

You may be quite conscious of your own disorganized state. You may wonder whether there is any way out of it. Just knowing that this is the common experience of widowhood, and that it is the usual prelude to reorganization of life can help you keep events and problems in perspective. But right now you may appreciate specific suggestions for accomplishing grief work.

3

Working Through Your Grief

Many writers stress the importance of grief work. But what is it, and how is it actually done? How can one work through the time of disorganization to reorganization and a so-called "steady state"? What is meant by a steady state?

Let us consider that last question first. The phrase "steady state" is borrowed from the natural sciences to express the desirable stability of the human being. A biologist might define it as a state of physiological equilibrium. A physicist might use the phrase "steady state" to describe an electrical system that can be stable under normal fluctuations of load or voltage.

Psychiatrist Karl Menninger defined the human steady state as that in which we try to "maintain relatively constant inner and outer environment by promptly correcting all upsetting eventualities."[7]

Think about the children's toy that is made to resemble a person whose lower extremities are inside a weighted ball. When a glancing blow knocks the figure sidewise, it always rights itself, to the endless delight and surprise of the youngster who hits it. An ordinary slap, or even the punch of a fist, is easily withstood. It comes back to a vertical position after each blow.

In somewhat similar style, you and I receive many of life's experiences with only brief upset, soon accommodating to events and circumstances. We keep relatively steady, despite various blows suffered. Only when great force and weight, such as bereavement, down us are we long delayed in regaining emotional equilibrium.

What are some of the specific things you can do to regain a steady state after your loss? The pouring out of sorrowful feelings is an urgent part of grief work. So also is ritualized mourning. Making the past history is vital to acceptance of widowhood status. There are people to thank, possessions to sort, business chores to do. Feelings of guilt need to be resolved, feelings of anger dealt with, in order that reorganization can take place.

Specifics of Grief Work

From my correspondence and interviews with widows, and from personal experience, the following notes on specifics of grief work are offered:

1. *Tears,* shed and unshed, are good indicators of what is happening, has happened, or may yet happen in bereavement reaction. For some widows it is hard to stop crying. They may struggle to regain control. But for many others there is that equally distressing problem—the unrelieved tension of "wishing I could cry."

You and those around you probably expected tears to flow at the time of the funeral, during supportive visits, and at the cemetery. But no one can predict the later tears that catch humans off guard. In unexpected ways, at unexpected times, fresh awareness of loss gives rise to tears.

When the seemingly small, inconsequential happenings trigger tears, you are a wise widow if you trust those who happen to observe to understand. You are even wiser to accept your own grief, your momentary release in tears, as natural rather than embarrassing.

A personal experience serves as an example. A month or so after my husband's death, we still had in the feedlot a steer he had selected for our own butchering and freezing. Something had to be done with the "prime" animal. A widow whose sons would be away in college wouldn't need much beef in her freezer. But parents living in the city and a neighbor couple were eager to buy part of the meat.

It was arranged to have the steer trucked to town for processing and packaging. In a week's time Parents H. and I made the journey to pick up our shares of the beef. After we had stored their portion, I set out for home.

About halfway home I felt unaccountably depressed. Tears made it difficult for me to see the road. As I finally reached our driveway, Carl's irreversible departure swept over me. I felt paralyzed, unable to act. How could I ever unload that meat and pack it into the freezer? We had always worked together at the job. He toted the heavy wire baskets. I handed him the packages to place in the deep, chest-type freezer. But it was not just slight physical stature that suddenly made the task overwhelming. The weakness and exhaustion of grief enervated me.

Shaking, I made my way to the telephone. The loyal neighbors, whose mourning for their daughter we had shared some years before, promptly answered. When they arrived to help, I ran to their arms—no longer ashamed of my need or my tears.

2. *The funeral and mourning rituals* are significant steps in grief work. By the time you read this, most or all of the rituals may have been carried out. No attempt will be made here to evaluate the widely varying kinds of funerals and memorial services.

You may agree with those who feel that the service should be a kind of testimony of faith. You may realize that it can and should be a stimulus to mourning.

Part of the reason for the service is to help you and others accept the pain of loss. It should also help you to begin an examination of your own life—to see your past in perspective, to contemplate your future.

Mourning rituals other than the funeral are also grief work

for many of us. These acts may be customary to our religious belief, to our community traditions, or to our family patterns. Creative individuals may originate ritual expressions compatible with their own ideas and emotions.

Your planning of a suitable furnishing for the church where your husband worshiped or a gift to a charity he believed in recognizes the worth of his life and the love of those who mourn.

When a funeral director placed one of those "In Memoriam" books in your hands, your initial reaction might have been that you don't want such a sad reminder. You may have shrunk from filling in the pages listing those who sent flowers, those who contributed memorials, those who helped serve meals to your family. You may have turned a page or two, looked at some signatures, and burst into tears.

But the simple work of adding names of those who cared enough to help is a step in acceptance. Gluing in the small cards that came with flowers, the news clippings, the list of neighbors who "went together" to give a memorial, is a healing task. Once the book is filled in, there is a sense of having walked another step away from the past, into the present and future.

3. *Review of the life.* By whatever method you do this, it is important grief work. Reviewing the earthly life of your mate may be accomplished in various ways. One form could be to reread a eulogy delivered at the funeral and tributes in written messages. Your family may review the life in conversation.

Later on, you may compose your own tribute to your mate. Some families like to share such thoughts in a Christmas letter or memorial folder. Material and format are matters for personal taste.

Adolescent or adult children sometimes appreciate the opportunity to express their tributes in prose or poetry. Even brief lines often carry deep significance. One need not be an experienced writer to be able to speak from the heart.

Those wise in the ways of sorrow remind us that it is important to recall *all* of the life with the one who died, the bad times as well as the good. Some of the painfulness of the bad memories will diminish during reminiscence.

We should bear in mind that persistent, obsessive review of death circumstances is quite different from needed review of the life. When a bereaved person continues to be preoccupied with details of the death event, professional care should be sought.

Some mothers of young children who have lost their father establish a memory corner in the living room or family room, with selected pictures and mementos to help them remember Daddy. Did your family take lots of snapshots? Arranging them in albums can help you review the life that was lived.

For her own interest and satisfaction, one widow wrote a summary of the work, activities, accomplishments, and pleasures she and her husband shared during his last year. It was a way of counting blessings and making the past history. Others have compiled scrapbooks recalling highlights of the married years. Some widows gather and record genealogical information, which serves to place individual human lives in perspective.

4. *Thank-yous—personal and meaningful.* It is true that the time for thank-yous coincides with the time when you are low on energy. The work may have to be spread out over weeks rather than days. But it is important work for you as you grieve, work that keeps you in contact with those who have demonstrated that they care.

The common practice of hurriedly mailing printed cards of thanks can deprive you of doing the task more slowly and thoughtfully. Family members and friends probably ought to confine their help to addressing and stamping the envelopes. If you desire to write a few lines of personal thanks, allow yourself time to do so, even though notes are somewhat delayed. People who honestly care are not waiting to be thanked anyway.

My helpful sister made a simple card file of all the caring folk who prepared food, sent flowers, gave memorials, or helped with farm chores. Many of the same people had aided me in several ways. As personal notes were written, specific kindness could be mentioned gratefully.

5. *Clothes and possessions*—their selective and sensible disposition. You may find it painful to give any of your husband's garments to persons who will wear them in your presence. Or you may be comfortable in bestowing clothing, watches, cameras, jewelry, or tools upon relatives or friends, and glad to see them used. You may want to be selective in retaining a few things with special significance or utilitarian value, while seeking new owners for items that will benefit others.

Remaining strongly attached to numerous articles of clothing and oddments of hobby paraphernalia may prevent accomplishment of grief work. On the other hand, an impulse to get rid of all reminders as quickly as possible may rush you through mourning too rapidly.

Charitable appeals for clothing and other articles provide used items to people who are needy. Why keep closets and drawers full of garments that could help others? Would your husband have approved of such hoarding? What is your own feeling about sharing? These are questions for you, the survivor, to answer and act upon.

6. *Drudgery* can be a blessing. When widows wrote me to tell what helped them progress from disorganization toward reorganization, they stressed the value of having to earn a living or apply themselves to business matters. Nearly all spoke, too, of such tasks as caring for the children, tending the garden, mowing the lawn, or rearranging the house furnishings as work that helped them through the weeks and months of grief. "My job was my salvation," "Gardening was my outlet," "The children's schedule kept me going," or "Regular work helps heal" were the kind of comments that came. As some put it, "Blessed be drudgery!" They are thankful for chores that help restore order in daily living.

Performing necessary tasks may at first seem distasteful and burdensome. But in the process of accomplishing such work, some of the past is reviewed and laid to rest.

7. *Resolving guilt and dealing with anger* is frequently part of grief work. Guilt may appear in various forms following the loss of a mate. Joan, a registered nurse, could not account for her inability to carry out first-aid procedures after her husband's collapse in a fatal heart attack. She was able to go to the telephone and summon the local rescue unit. But she was too dazed to perform emergency acts she had known and practiced for years.

Months after the death, Joan still felt serious guilt. She went over and over the circumstances, wondering how she could have failed to take note of her husband's vague symptoms during the day preceding the attack. But mostly she blamed herself for being unequal to what she conceived of as an emergency in which there might have been some hope of recovery. The physician's assurances that first-aid measures would not have saved her husband did not convince her. She began to resolve her guilt only when she learned of other widows' similar experiences and feelings.

Anger toward his deceased wife's doctor was a dominant emotion for Roy. The doctor had been so preoccupied with his own marital troubles that he did not recognize Mary Ellen's definite symptoms, which called for diagnostic testing.

By the time another physician was placed in charge of the case, the cancer had metastasized. Some of Roy's anger was turned back toward himself. Why had he not asked a second medical opinion earlier, when the cancer was treatable? Talking through the whole course of events with two impartial hearers helped Roy to take a calmer view, essential to his progress in grief work.

Anger is sometimes a part of grief because it has been part of a marriage. But it also occurs when marriage has been quite happy. You may feel anger at being left behind, at being left with heavy responsibilities, at being left to rear the children alone, at being left with a mountain of debt. Admitting the anger, at least privately, and praying for strength to deal with it may be among your important steps in working through your grief.

Working through guilt or anger successfully often requires professional care. Those who have lost mates through suicide may need special understanding and handling. So also do those whose mates have died as the result of their habits and excesses.

"You never get over it," is the positive-sounding statement of many widows. In one sense it is true. The loss of a spouse becomes forever a part of life experience, always having its effect upon what comes afterward. But in another sense the "never" is some widows' way of proclaiming their love and loyalty. Even when they say "you never get over it," most widows know that the pain of separation is diminished over a period of time.

You and I cannot expect everyone to realize that grief work is a process to be understood and carried through, in order that the steady state can be regained. But, as individuals, we can learn its value for ourselves and for others who are bereaved.

You will be wise to recognize that the time needed to work through grief varies considerably. Mourning is not completed until you have adjusted adequately to a world without your husband. Once the initial phase of shock and numbness and the much longer phase of disorganization have been weathered, you will find yourself able to transfer love and interest from your lost spouse to other persons.

Believing that one's grief will always dominate and control future thoughts and actions is bound to be self-destructive. Suppression and repression are just as unhealthy. But when we know the phases of grief, when we allow and encourage their expression, we make possible the integration of bereavement experience into our surprisingly adaptable selves.

Self-Help Groups

A number of self-help groups for widows have sprung up in recent years. Some have been founded by those whose own bereavement experiences have enabled them to empathize with the newly widowed. Others were organized to give help while at the same time engaging in research. And who knows how many local, informal meetings of widows there are, where a few people have felt a common need?

Brief sketches of several groups about which information has been gathered are presented:

The *Widow-to-Widow Program* was developed by researchers at the Harvard Medical School Laboratory of Community Psychiatry with trained volunteers who had experienced widowhood. Begun in 1968 in the Boston area, it was later supported by Action for Independent Maturity (AIM).

The program "was an experiment to test the feasibility of another widow becoming a care giver to the newly widowed. It was hypothesized that she would be able to use her own experience to help others, that her special empathy would enable her to understand the support needed, that she could accept the new widow's distress over an extended period of time, and that she would be accepted if she offered her assistance to the new widow."[8]

The Widow-to-Widow Program tried to reach all widowed women under age sixty in a given community. Realizing that the newly bereaved person is confused and unsure of needs, the care givers sought out the widows. Often the one making the contact went as a neighbor or friend who had had similar bereavement. Much work has also been done over the twenty-four-hour Widowed Service telephone line. The widow aide has provided support, served as a role model, and been a "bridge person" back into the real world.

Specific ways in which aides have helped the widowed include: exchange of common feelings; making the transition from wife to widow; finding local groups with common interests in travel, recreation, study, etc.; finding car pools or obtaining driver education; facing rather than running from new reality.

Groups have followed such a plan in San Francisco, California; Ann Arbor, Michigan; Mechanicsburg, Pennsylvania; and Waukesha, Wisconsin. Information can be obtained from Widowed Persons Service, Action for Independent Maturity, 1225 Connecticut Avenue, N.W., Washington, D.C. 20036.

A *Widowed Persons Service* is operated by the American Association of Retired Persons (AARP) at a number of locations. Volunteer counselors give guidance in coping with grief, dealing with financial matters, making important decisions, knowing when to postpone decisions, confronting loneliness and fears, and finding employment. Information about this service and locations where it is available may be obtained by writing: Widowed Persons Service, AARP, 1909 K Street, N.W., Washington, D.C. 20049.

The Solitaires, an organization for widows in Omaha, Nebraska, was started by Mary Brite. She views her personal ministry to widows as "letting women know that God loves them," emphasizing that when all a widow's professional helpers, relatives, and friends have left, she still has God with her.

Solitaires are women of many ages, faiths, and stages of grief. They get together to share monthly, in whatever stage of grief or adjustment they currently find themselves. Meetings combine informational and social features. Buzz groups limited to three or four women carry on discussion after a topic is presented. Members' addresses and telephone numbers are given only to members of the group, not to outsiders who may exploit widows.

Churches provide meeting space for Omaha Solitaires. In Sioux City, Iowa, a similar group, with permission from the Omaha group to use the name "Solitaires," began in 1977 to meet at the Women's Center on the campus of Briar Cliff College.

The Widows Consultation Center counsels women from all social, ethnic, and financial backgrounds, primarily residents of the New York Metropolitan area. Located at 136 East 57th Street, New York, N.Y. 10022, the Center has received correspondence from over the nation, indicating that more such centers are needed.

Founded in 1970, and supported by a grant from the Prudential Insurance Company of America, the Widows Consultation Center is nonsectarian, nonprofit, and staffed by experienced professional advisers.

The THEOS Foundation, 11609 Frankstown Road, Pittsburgh, Pa. 15235, has chapters in many states and in Canada. Through the efforts of Bea Decker, this organization, offering spiritually enriched educational programs for the widowed and their families, held its first meeting February 25, 1962, with sixty-five persons from Pennsylvania and Ohio attending.

According to Mrs. Decker, the main objective of THEOS (the letters stand for "They Help Each Other Spiritually") is to help men and women make the major transition into singlehood by helping them rebuild their lives with Christ as a foundation. Local chapters are advised to reach out constantly for the newly bereaved and to gear their program to young and middle-aged widows and widowers.

Until 1975, THEOS chapters were chartered simply by signifying their intent to form and by submitting a letter of intent from the sponsoring church. Since then, an annual charter fee of one hundred dollars has been required, to help defray newsletter and other costs, also to demonstrate financial support by members, necessary to qualify THEOS for foundation grants.

THEOS Foundation provides pamphlets and books for the widowed at nominal cost on a nonprofit basis. A proper balance of the four elements of a good Christian program is advised: worship, education, fellowship, and service.

THEOS social activity is family-oriented. THEOS recommends that members become average citizens of their communities, participating in life with outside groups.

Parents Without Partners International is a nonprofit, nonsectarian, educational organization devoted exclusively to the welfare and interests of single parents and their children. It serves widowed, divorced, separated, and never-married parents who are willing to join together for mutual help.

Organized in 1957, PWP has basically educational purposes and uses professional help. Some of the recreational activities are planned for adults, and some for members with their families. While some PWP discussion groups may be chiefly for the widowed, and others for the divorced or separated, many of the programs address the needs of all single-parent homes.

A new PWP chapter may be formed with a minimum of fifteen members. Where information is not locally available, interested persons may send inquiries to Parents Without Partners International, 7910 Woodmont Avenue, Washington, D.C. 20014.

Spontaneous local widows' groups may arise when a few widows in a community feel a need to get together for sharing of their feelings, problems, and ways of coping. Most of these have from four to eight members, who meet once a week or once a month. Conversation on subjects of special interest to widows and occasional social evenings out are the main activities.

One such group was formed by eight women, widowed in their middle years. They decided not to increase their number as new widows appeared in the community, but to encourage new groups of similar kind and size, for intimate communication. Marriage would automatically terminate membership in the group.

Should you investigate and perhaps join a self-help group? If you think you might benefit from exchanging ideas with others facing similar change in their lives, the time may be ripe for you to find or to help organize such a group in your area. Many widows report that they are working through grief and restructuring their lives more effectively because they have frequent contact with those who are learning to deal with bereavement.

4

Overcoming Loneliness and Isolation

Almost every woman who loses her husband by death has some fear that she cannot handle life without her mate. This feeling comes to those who still have children in the home, and to those who share living quarters with relatives, as well as to those who are living alone.

Much of the fear of loneliness is really the fear of having no sure place in the scheme of things. It is the fear, not the loneliness, that incapacitates you for carrying out your new responsibilities and finding the new direction of your life.

As a wife you probably knew your role quite well. It may have been challenging, varied, sometimes frustrating, but often fulfilling. At first glance you may think widowhood looks futile, hopeless, useless, empty. Is it possible to function in a widow role and not be burdened with loneliness anxiety?

Some widows, convinced they cannot stand being alone, have told me how they try to evade their fear. In some cases they make their older children feel that the widowed mother "must" have someone with her almost constantly, and especially at night. Others deliberately assume an unreasonably heavy work load, so that they "will not have time to think." A number remark that the presence of an animal pet, or the continual playing of stereo music, gives them a sense of someone-in-the-house, which keeps them from panicking.

Nearly all widows speak of the difficulty they have in cooking and eating alone, sleeping alone, making decisions alone, attending events alone. If you have never been alone, you may think the aloneness is the sole cause of your loneliness anxiety.

Widowhood may be the first solitary state you have ever known. Did you go directly from your parents' home into your married home? If you attended college or earned your living prior to marriage, did you always have a roommate? Were you and your husband a very "close" couple? The change from sharing life intimately to going-it-alone may be quite threatening, and adjusting to it will take time. You will need to "think" the change before you can make the transition.

Values in Loneliness

To develop an appreciation for loneliness rather than to succumb to it may be your big challenge. Clark Moustakas, author of well-known books on loneliness, has observed: "To see is to be lonely, to hear, feel, touch—every vital, solitary experience of the senses is a lonely one. Anyone who senses with a wide range of delicate feelings and meanings experiences loneliness. To be open to life in an authentic sense is to be lonely."[9]

The same author has pointed out that loneliness enables. It "enables one to return to a life with others with renewed hope and vitality, with a fuller dedication, with a deeper desire to come to a healthy resolution of problems and issues involving others, with possibility and hope for a rich, true life with others. . . .

"When one has felt totally forlorn, desolate, and abandoned, one can arrive at a new depth of companionship and a new sense of joy and belonging. . . . Let there be loneliness, for where there is loneliness, there also is love, and where there is suffering, there also is joy."[10]

Discoveries about loneliness can be eye-opening. Take a better look at some of the reasons why many men and women choose to live alone. This may be the first time in your life that you have been in a position to understand their feelings. If you deeply resent a singlehood you did not choose, it may be quite a revelation to learn that some others have different views of what is a desirable state.

In *The Wonderful Crisis of Middle Age,* Eda LeShan reminds us, "There is really only one companion that one can count on all through one's life—oneself; that needs to be a meaningful and satisfying friendship."[11] And Isabella Taves, in *Women Alone,* declares, "There are moments when it is bliss to go home and close the door and not have to account to anybody!"[12]

How about the value that creative persons see in solitude? For example, think of Thoreau, who "never found the companion that was so companionable as solitude"; of Thomas Edison, who isolated himself much of the time while working on his inventions; or of the composer Handel, who shut himself in his lodgings to write the oratorio *The Messiah.* Name almost any highly creative woman or man, and you name a person who appreciated loneliness, who required a measure of solitude.

The women I know who accept singleness readily tend to be the same ones who know that "to love is to be lonely." They recognize that human love is destined to be broken by separation or by death. Loss and grief are certain to come sometime, they say. They may have been short on solitude during busy child-rearing years, and oversupplied in widowhood. But they intend to accept the condition when it comes and make the most of their opportunities.

I cannot go along with those who say we must *fight* loneliness. Recognizing that loneliness is a part of life experience, and taking it to ourselves as part of our growth, enables us to overcome loneliness anxiety. Separation from the mate who has shared one's life in many ways does leave the survivor lonely, even if not dwelling alone. But a new togetherness of spirit is possible. Jo Pullen expressed such thought and feeling in her poem:

SEPARATION

All whom I love
I bind to myself
with ribbons longer
than the world,
And so I need not
hold them close
but send them flying free,
knowing that when
or wherever they go,
a slender shining filament
links them to me.[13]

Besides having a sense of continuing companionship with the departed spouse in a spiritual way, widows often find a reservoir of loving concern in the community. While living alone on the farm after my husband's death, I was fortunate to be in a neighborhood of people who did care. Even when busy schedules meant that days and weeks went by without seeing some of them face-to-face, I was made aware of their friendship.

I learned that some of them took kindly note of my goings and comings, observing whether I was out gardening or mowing, seeing my light at night. Some who seldom took time for a chat were quick to lend a hand with heating problems during a blizzard.

For the Christian, there is a model for valuing loneliness in the life of Jesus, and an assurance of never being without God's companionship.

Taking some positive steps with regard to your emerging life-style in widowhood is a good way to overcome the fear of loneliness. Are you creating a setting suited to your tastes, interests, and need for security? Is your home becoming more yours as a single person, or yours as a one-parent family? Are you altering the arrangement of furniture, especially the pieces that had been arranged primarily for your husband's comfort and convenience? Are you thinking now of what appeals to you, and to your children if they are still in the home?

If security is one of your chief concerns, have you satisfied your need to have good locks on doors and windows, to take all recommended measures for safety? Have you moved on to other important matters with reasonable peace of mind?

Have you begun to cultivate a cheerful atmosphere through decor? Have you considered new friends as well as old in the arrangement of facilities for entertaining? Have you kept in mind your own needs for privacy? Have you thought of your home as one from which you can reach out to others who are lonely?

It helps to know that you can quickly be in touch with people you love when you have the need. A thoughtful son insisted that I have an extension telephone beside my bed, in my upstairs room at the farm, when I began living alone. It would provide a measure of security in case of illness or other emergency. It would also make communication with family and friends easy.

As a matter of fact, the telephone often went unused while I read books and magazines from the stack always close at hand, while I meditated, prayed, reviewed the past, and planned for the future. But it was comforting to know that beloved humans would answer a dialed number if I needed to call.

Learning from people who make the most of singlehood, or from anyone who accepts and uses periods of solitude, is another positive step you may take. A good number of my most "alive" and adventurous friends are single people. When I talk with them, I hear about their current creative interests, their exciting travel preparation, their enthusiasm for new learning. As a widow, you may come, as I did, to appreciate opportunities for unpressured planning or chosen activity.

It may be something of a surprise to reach a new level of commitment and dedication to personal goals *because* you have been experiencing both aloneness and loneliness. As you overcome your fears of having no place in life and no one to care, you may want to channel some energies toward others' needs. You may now have more concern about loving others than being loved!

Your Feelings of Social Isolation

A forty-four-year-old widow once wrote in desperation to "Dear Abby." The woman's husband had died of a lingering illness, leaving her with three children—two teen-age boys and a daughter twelve years old. Friends and relatives had lavished attention upon the bereaved family. The last thing the widow heard from each of them was, "If you need anything, please call me."

In her letter the widow declared: "Abby, I need *everything.* I need someone to take an interest in two teen-aged boys who have no father. I need someone to cheer me up when I'm feeling low. I need someone to dress up for. I need someone to get me out of the house and invite me to a movie, a bridge game, a play, a concert, or an evening of conversation so I will know I'm alive. A widow needs everything any other normal woman needs, but she can't call up her friends and ask them for anything."[14]

Why couldn't the widow wipe out her feelings of social isolation by calling her friends and asking them for the help she needed? They had promised to supply her needs. They had urged her to call, had they not?

Some would say pride prevented the widow's calling her friends. But those who have looked inside widowhood would more likely name loss of self-esteem, coupled with her growing suspicion that friends had mouthed a promise they did not expect to have claimed. Have you sometimes felt the same way about your well-meaning friends' offers to "help" you?

If you wait for friends to come to the rescue, you may have

to wait indefinitely. Yet some who themselves have known bereavement may make a point of staying in touch. And others not bereaved but unusually sensitive to persons' needs may reach out to you. Whether their overtures will meet with responsiveness on your part will probably be determined by your progress in accepting loss and change as facts of your life.

It will help to know some of the positive steps that may enable you to handle better your feelings of being left out, forgotten, ignored, or cut off from couple-oriented recreations you formerly enjoyed. To begin with, you might try taking a closer look at the origin of some of the feelings.

Your New Unwanted Role

If your reactions are like mine, you will find yourself disliking the very term "widow," wishing there were a substitute word that would somehow soften the reality. You may complain that you are "a left-over nothing," that you "feel amputated," or that you now understand the full import of that worn-out phrase "being a fifth wheel." Yet you may not be able to bring yourself to say to anyone for a while: "I am a widow." Avoiding the word, you tend to reject your unsought, unwanted new role.

An example will show my loss of self-esteem in an early stage of bereavement. When my husband Carl was alive, we always sat in a pew toward the front of the church. Because he served a monthly stint as an usher each year, he empathized with those responsible for seating worshipers. Many people tried to squeeze into the rear pews. Carl convinced me and our sons that we could encourage those who hung back by sitting farther forward. Gradually we developed a sense of indicating enthusiastic support of the church in this way.

On the first Sunday after the death of their father, the boys were still home from college. They attended the morning worship service with me, and we sat near the front. But on the Sundays following I slipped into as inconspicuous a seat as I could find, near the back, usually beside some other "woman alone." If an usher attempted to lead me farther forward, I shook my head and gestured toward a rear seat I had noticed was empty.

My church attendance continued to be regular. I did not feel glad and proud to be in the congregation, the way I used to as Carl's wife. I felt sorry for myself, having to go alone. To tell the truth, I felt like hiding—like sitting behind the folding door in the fellowship hall, listening to the sermon on the PA system, and leaving without shaking hands or greeting a soul.

Sometimes I gave myself a mental scolding, observing how much better my lot was than other widowed persons of the congregation. Financially secure, able to continue and expand my work as a writer, possessed of a comfortable home and a dependable car, and comparatively at ease about sons who were both in college, I had many pluses others lacked. If I viewed my situation fairly, there was no justification for self-pity.

To recognize and admit the loss of one's self-esteem is a part of widowhood experience. Confusion about one's worth as a single person, when for so long identity came with and through a husband, is understandable.

Pointing out that a man's self-worth lies in his work, the money he has, or the power he wields, Isabella Taves, in *Women Alone,* declares that a woman's self-worth often resides in her husband. She tells of a doctor's wife who was given great consideration during the years when her husband served the community. Although the doctor's practice frequently prevented his attendance at social and cultural events, people saw to it that his wife was provided with transportation and given preferential treatment.

She was important to the community because her husband was an essential person. After her husband's death, the physician's wife felt she had "turned into nothing." As she tartly observed, the wife of the new doctor was now the one getting all the attention!

Change in You and Your Friends

You may have found as I did that some of your friends unconsciously altered their view of you when you became a widow. They may still be finding it difficult, if not impossible, to relate to you in your strange new role. Communication may be strained.

As one widow's friend expressed it: "I don't know what to say. . . . I never mention her loss. . . . I try to keep from talking about what happened. . . . I feel awkward about facing her, so I put off going to see her or asking her over. . . . I don't think we're ever going to have the friendship we used to have. . . . I'm sorry, but I just don't know *how* to talk with a widow."

It is equally hard for the widow. More than a year after her husband's death, a widow wrote: "I am still not at ease when there are married people in my presence. I force myself to attend weddings, funerals, and social gatherings, but I always feel 'very alone' and even awkward. I have accepted that relatives and friends, especially married ones, neither come to my house nor invite me to their homes in the same way they did before."

Pat D., a widow in her thirties, had it figured out that friends stayed away because they didn't want to become involved in possible repair work and maintenance of her home. She may have been right. She decided to make it clear that she would either accomplish such tasks herself or hire them done.

Nataline L. observed that when she specifically invited friends, they showed up. But she thought she detected a lack of enthusiasm on their part. Was she too sensitive, she wondered? Was she imagining that her friends came out of a sense of duty? Was it best to release them from any obligation, and look for new friendships?

A few months after I was widowed, our county had its annual All-Extension Banquet. Currently I was serving on the extension council, representing our township, so it was expected that I would support the event. Many of our neighbors were going, but apparently none thought to offer me a ride. I was widow-shy about mentioning the banquet to any of them. I did not want to be in the position of hinting for a ride, and I knew that rural men are not eager to have a woman do the chauffering.

I drove my car some twenty miles to the banquet location, feeling my aloneness. I felt conspicuous all evening, acutely conscious of my late husband's absence, especially when a certificate of recognition for his project leadership was presented posthumously. When the program ended, I rushed to my car and drove home in an agitated state.

Though I had been among many good friends, who greeted me solicitously, undeniably I had hostile feelings. I know now that my anger had been generated by my sense of abandonment by my husband. Quite unreasonably, I was blaming folks at the banquet for my social discomfort.

How are you dealing with the hazards in social relationships during widowhood? You may be fortunate in having "couple friends" who stand by you and take you places frequently. Have you come to expect them to include you every time? Are you hurt if they don't invite you? Have you ever tried to imagine the situation reversed? What if you were *expected* to invite the same friend every time? Would you much prefer to be free to bestow kindnesses when you felt the impulse?

If you are sensitive to others' feelings, you will realize that women friends, even dear friends, *do* feel threatened by a widow. In some wives' views, husbands who are genuinely sympathetic and kind toward the bereaved may need to be protected from possible temptation. This can be a wifely feeling even when "complete trust" is expressed!

In the early weeks and months of bereavement you may have turned thankfully to a woman friend—perhaps an unattached woman—for needed companionship. It is easy to become too dependent during this time of mourning, and to let yourself believe that the friend should be continually available for listening, for advice, for accompanying you to meetings, and even to business appointments.

Some women friends with good intentions may step in to dominate your choice of social contacts. You may find that unless you take initiative to maintain control of your comings and goings, you will be locked into a schedule you did not choose. Because you need attention, you may let yourself in for involvements without full awareness of the implications. It may seem strange to warn widows to guard against friendship that smothers. But when one has not yet learned to value solitude, vulnerability is high.

The really priceless friend is the one who wants what is best for you. She wants you to be able to enjoy sharing some social life, but also to be capable of going alone part of the time. She wants you to have some breadth and some depth in your human relationships. She wants to be near during the time when you truly need someone to talk with, but she also wants you to develop your own spiritual resources for sustenance.

In widowhood you may have discovered that you need understanding women friends more than you have ever needed them. Being a contributor as well as a recipient in these relationships can stimulate personal growth. But limiting yourself to friendships with women stops short of the desirable balance in having friendships with men as well.

A woman widowed at age fifty wrote: "Since childhood I have enjoyed the company of men, and so that relationship was sadly missed. Oh, I flew [she had earned her pilot's license] with many men, and was considered 'one of the guys,' but except for a few who liked to include me, I was a social outcast —a fifth wheel, anyway. I got so bored with woman talk and most of all, gossip. So after the initial shock, that was undoubtedly the most difficult adjustment to make. This doesn't mean that I don't enjoy women, but much as I like chocolate cake, I don't want it three times a day."

Although you may not be ready to consider dating, you can keep in touch with the world of men and women through service on boards and committees, through political action, through volunteer work. Contacts with men in these ways will probably be friendly but businesslike. You will be spared self-consciousness which might arise in a contrived situation.

Continuing to serve on councils and committees in the community proved deeply satisfying to me. I felt at home in these meetings where policy-making was carried on by concerned men and women. It was comfortable to be in these mixed groups where there were no couples and no particular attention paid to anyone's sex.

Being part of discussions in which both men and women expressed their views provided desirable change from several all-feminine groups I belonged to. My input at council meetings seemed minimal to me, but how intellectually stimulating and companionable council members were! Without knowing it, they supplied essential support for my efforts to establish a new personal identity!

In widowhood you will probably find yourself reorganizing your friendships. At first I had no idea how much my friendships might be tested, and in some instances altered. But almost instinctively I felt I should no longer plan to be a member of the one small social group to which Carl and I went only as a couple.

Bless their hearts, these longtime friends pressed me to continue in the supper-and-bridge club as a widow. We could invite a guest each time to be my bridge partner, they assured me.

But I considered the perennial problem for the hosts, and the precedent that would be set. Sometime another death would occur. If it left another widow, the club would soon be "uncoupled." Perhaps I was also motivated by fear of pain involved in going alone to a group we had enjoyed so much as a pair.

"I'll be willing to come as a guest now and then, but I won't be a member," I declared. How relieved I was, as time passed, and how relieved I think they have been, that the decision to drop membership set us all free! The couples in the club have continued to be my good friends, though I have many new friends and interests. I think they understood my need to change during widowhood.

People who are growing are people who are reorganizing their friendships in keeping with circumstances, needs, and common interests. Instead of clutching at faithful friends, and perhaps becoming dependent upon them, widows need to try their wings among some new companions.

5

Your Bereaved Children

Children are often labeled "a comfort" to a bereaved parent. "They are all I have left of Joe," or "They help keep my mind off my own grief," may be the way you have expressed this feeling. When young arms embrace you tightly, and small bodies tremble against yours, you are grateful for the sharing of grief. When you have to attend to the urgent needs of your offspring, you may recognize the value of the efforts as an antidote to despondency.

But all too soon, the trials of single parenthood begin to appear. You may still be feeling too upset, too deserted, to face such heavy responsibility with composure and confidence. Yet somehow you have to act.

The question of the child's attendance at the funeral of his or her parent has naturally drawn the attention of those who have studied and written about children's mourning. The consensus is to encourage school-age children to attend, but not to urge or force them to be present.

Sharing the family experience can help your child to mourn in an atmosphere of loving concern. Having details of the service and burial explained in advance prepares the child to understand the customs of honoring the deceased.

If your child chooses not to attend the funeral, make arrangements for him to remain at home with an adult friend. A private visit to the funeral home, and a later visit to the grave, will help the child understand the physical realities of death.

A child who does not want to attend the funeral or memorial service may indicate denial of the death of his parent. A perceptive parent or other adult who is close to the child may be able to encourage discussion and questioning that will help him accept the fact of death.

It is not surprising if the bereaved child has a change of mind and decides to share the funeral experience with the family. But whether or not this occurs, the need for help in accepting the death is urgent. In all the confusion of the household, this important need should not be overlooked. If you realize belatedly that a child in your family continues to deny the death that occurred some time ago, you will need to recognize the situation. You will also need to give or secure help.

Some parents who have trouble with their own attitudes may confess that they find it hard to go to the funeral home, or to see the body in the casket, yet convey to the child that most people do deal with such matters more comfortably. In the face of questions you have trouble in answering, a move for assistance from another adult is indicated.

Your child may be wondering about the appearance of the casket and the father's body. How does Daddy look when he is dead? What clothes is he wearing? Is he lying down? How big is a casket?

A visit to the funeral home with you or another trusted adult should answer most such questions, and may assure the child of the restful appearance of the dead father. A basis for further communication may be laid by the visit if it is well conducted.

Expect to hear repeated questions such as: Where did Daddy go? Why did Daddy leave us? What does dead mean? It is especially trying to answer when you are feeling the deep pain of your own loss. Yet the children need help in order to accept the finality of Father's leaving.

If you are secure in a religious belief that does not blame

God for tragedy, you can probably convey that faith to the child. If you are honest, your child will not be told such fictions as "Daddy is away on a long trip" or "He just went to sleep" or "God took him because he was good." Your child should not be told things that you do not accept yourself. Answer honestly, even if the answer is "I don't know."

Lucille F., a widow of twelve years, recalled that visits she and her youngsters made to the father's grave aided the whole family's acceptance of the death. She and the children observed the stone marker, thought about and talked about Dad, watched boats on the nearby ocean, and shared quiet time in a peaceful place. When they moved to the Midwest, they kept the memory of those visits to the grave.

In some instances, a parent who is expecting death may actually be able to help prepare the child for the experience, even to understanding the function of a cemetery. My own sons made their first trip to a cemetery on Memorial Day with their paternal grandmother. She had cancer, and knew she would not likely live more than a few months. The boys were six and seven years of age at the time.

Grandmother B. led the lads to the graves of her parents and other family members, quietly explaining that their bodies had been buried when they no longer had use for them. She sang the words of an old hymn, in the original German, as it appeared on the sides of the monument marking the graves of those who came as immigrants to the United States.

Meanwhile Grandfather was noticing the several varieties of prairie wild flowers, which he pointed out when the hymn was concluded. Together the grandparents talked with their grandsons about how the land had been set aside long ago for use as a cemetery. They recalled that many members of the families who had started the church nearby had been buried in the plots provided.

In a few months, when Grandmother B. died, the boys attended the funeral service and went along to the cemetery.

They had assurance that the rites were fitting. Appreciation of that early opportunity to learn of death and burial was registered years later. When they suddenly lost their father in accidental death, a foundation for integrating loss had been laid. They were fortunate that the childhood experience was directed by two adults with firm religious conviction and compassion.

Care of the Children

If you are temporarily unable to carry out all of your maternal functions, other adults are needed to help care for younger children in your bereaved family. True understanding and appropriate supportive action are invaluable during this period. You may rather readily resume your mother role, but find that you struggle with those added aspects of parenthood which "Daddy" formerly fulfilled.

Ordinary tasks of laundry, cooking, grocery shopping, and cleaning loom as heavy burdens when accustomed strength is lacking. When you are drained of physical and emotional energy, unable to perform the most elementary homemaking tasks, how can you rise to the unpredictable demands of parenting?

From your child's point of view, to have lost Father, and at the same time to have had a great change occur in Mother, is almost too much. It is especially important in dealing with bereaved children to remember that change in one person in a role network is bound to affect everyone in the network. If you and the other adults close to the child are aware of this, you are better able to understand the child's situation.

Not only you and the children have been changed by loss. Grandparents, also grieving, may suddenly be called upon to share your responsibility for child-rearing. Or, in reversed consequences of the death, paternal grandparents may as suddenly be cut off from a formerly close relationship with the children. Is careful thought being given to the needs of the persons involved?

Who will the helper or helpers be, if you require assistance with child care and homemaking? Is there a relative willing and able to undertake this work for the time when you are recovering strength, attending to extraordinary tasks connected with the loss of your husband, and striving to reorganize family living? If not, there may be a dedicated friend who will offer such aid. Or a suitable paid helper may be found.

Homemaker Service now available in many parts of the country can be a godsend to your bereaved family. Often the need is for temporary help—to bring into the home a capable and understanding person who will be both supportive and, if need be, instructive. Such a Homemaker can help bridge the gap between the period of confusion and the time when relative stability is achieved. Strengthening and improving family life is one of the goals of Homemaker Service.

Awareness of the Child's Circumstances

During many of his or her waking hours, your bereaved child may be in charge of a sitter. You may be working at a job outside the home, perhaps for the first time. The child's brothers and sisters may compete more intensely for your attention than when they had a father, too. Some of the adults your child previously counted upon to be poised and understanding may have become short-tempered, preoccupied, or self-concerned.

The hikes and other kinds of outings formerly taken with Dad may be altogether lacking, just when such shared recreation would aid relaxation and communication. Fatherly interest and approval are now missing. Dad's authority can no longer be tested and accepted.

Little wonder that your bereaved child may suffer insomnia, have temper tantrums, regress in toilet training, eat compulsively, become aggressive, or feel great anxiety lest he himself or his surviving parent also die!

You may not have recognized the child's possible feeling that he is a liability to you. Have you complained about the expense or inconvenience of using a sitter, so that you can earn outside the home? Have you given the impression that the child hampers your social life, is "in the way," or is "a problem"?

It is not unusual to be blind to signs of children's mourning. At the same time, you may expect more mature consideration and helpfulness from them than they are capable of giving. You know you have suffered a great loss, but you may be less aware of your children's grief.

My own memory of bereavement includes instances of this kind. Though able to make the two telephone calls to my sons away at college, informing them of their father's accidental death, and to cry with them when they arrived at the hospital, I was insensitive later on to some of the ways in which they manifested grief. This was partly because of preoccupation with many unaccustomed duties, but also because of my limited understanding of mourning.

When the son who had formerly shown great interest in our herd and other farm operations exhibited some strangely negative attitudes toward necessary chores, I chided him. I mentioned his father's untiring labors. Much later, the thought occurred that doing alone those very tasks—once shared so comfortably with Dad—must have accentuated Dale's feeling of loss.

His sudden abandonment of pheasant- and duck-hunting as a much-enjoyed hobby also bewildered me. How could I tactfully explain to kind friends—some his own age and some his Dad's age—who offered to include him in their hunting expeditions, why Dale didn't want to go? I had not yet recognized that quitting the sport previously enjoyed in company with Dad could be a way of mourning.

Your younger child's need for a stable adult to help him

mourn can scarcely be overemphasized. Such an adult will be compassionate and patient in giving simple answers to questions that the child may keep repeating until he is satisfied. Overexplaining—answering questions not really asked—ought to be avoided.

If the lost parent died in an accident, the child will need to learn that accidents happen, and we have to endure the results. If you urged your children to pray for their father when he was sick, without preparing them for the possibility that he might not recover, you have a difficult assignment. How will you explain to the children that "it was all for the best" when their father died, despite their prayers? Your own understanding of prayer will have to be examined.

It is my observation that if you are struggling to accept and account for the death, you had best confess your own bewilderment to your children. If you do this, you may also be able to assure the children that they can expect to be strengthened, comforted, and helped toward greater understanding. Genuine religious faith can be most helpful, even when death mysteries remain.

Praying together in an open and receptive mood can be strengthening for both you and your child. Reading aloud together selected passages of Scripture and appropriate children's literature may increase understanding of life and death. Such reading may also aid your child in verbalizing his grief and questions.

Stages and Signs of Children's Grief

The stages of grief and the tasks to accomplish are much the same for your children and you:

1. Reality of separation and loss must be fully accepted and recognized.

2. Painful and distressing feelings that accompany the loss must be felt and shared.

3. Attachment to the loved (lost) person must be surrendered so that the self may be invested in new relationships.[15]

Fuller understanding of what grief means in the life of each child, depending upon his or her level of development and his or her personality, can be gained if you observe carefully. Be prepared to take cues from the child, to read and become informed on children's grief, and to consult with resource persons.

While some children may go through stages of mourning in a few weeks, others take much longer. The sooner the child can be helped to acknowledge permanent loss, the sooner progress through his mourning can occur.

Like your adult mourning, the child's grief may show up in protest, despair, and detachment at various times. Early protest may burst out in weeping and temper tantrums. Later, while the child is still oriented to the lost parent, his longing for the one who died and his hostility toward those who would help may be apparent. Healing has taken place when the child is able to seek an attachment to a new person.

Edgar Jackson, clergyman and author of books on grief, has pointed out that unless a child has learned to accept deprivation when adults say "no" to relatively small things, he will be "desperately resistant when a big 'No' comes along in the form of the death of someone he loves." The same writer notes that the child's reaction will also depend much upon the ideas of death he has gathered, the explanations he has rèceived about the deaths of pets or other animals.

But as Jackson puts it: "Most of all . . . [the child] will be influenced by the expression of feelings of the adults around him. If he encounters only hysteria and collapse and nagging recrimination, he will naturally be over-wrought and frightened, because in addition to his own feelings of loss he is suffering the panic of seeing grownups go to pieces.

"If a family talks with composure, explaining to children in language they can understand that someone they love is not going to be there any more, the child accepts the quiet expression and responds in similar fashion."[16]

The "big No" has to be comprehended. Leading a child to think of the father's absence as only temporary not only is dishonest but also may be dangerous for emotional health. Evasive and inadequate answers will lead to more questioning, or to fears and worries that are worse than the loss itself.

The explanation often given when an elderly person dies, that the body is now worn out and no longer useful to the person, is acceptable to the child. Not so, the attempted explanation of a younger person's untimely death on a similar basis. When the child's parent has died, the logic of death at an advanced age is obviously inappropriate.

If you convey to your children the knowledge that grief is a constructive experience to go through, painful though it is, you are on the way to aiding both their progress and your own. Crying together, expressing feelings of loss, and confessing that one cannot make all necessary adjustments quickly, or easily, should be considered natural. How important it is to be honest, and admittedly in need of help, from God and from persons!

If you can say aloud: "I miss Daddy so much today. . . . It seems he will surely come driving home from work and hurry into the house for supper, . . . but I know it won't happen," the children may also be able to talk of their feelings: "I wish Daddy could be here to play with us at night the way he used to be. . . . I'd be as good as gold." Such fantasy helps exercise emotions, yet differentiates between wishes and realities.

Fears, nightmares, aggressive actions, or digestive instability are common signs of a child's grief. For a time the child may feel anger toward the doctor, toward God, or toward the dead father he thinks has abandoned him. He may theorize that his own bad actions caused the father's death, and feel burdened with guilt. Or he may have an obsession with the father's good qualities. The child may try to become head of the family, and his mother's substitute mate.

With the best of intentions you or another adult may demand of the child, "You have to be the man of the house!" Or, "You will have to take care of your mother from now on!" Suddenly it is assumed that a child can and should take on a grown-up role. Yet taking on adult responsibilities may cut off natural growth. The child may be kept from his own mourning process. Thrust forward to undertake work and decisions for which he is not yet equipped, he is robbed of part of his personal development.

This is certainly not to say that children should be denied the sharing of appropriate homemaking tasks. Such experience is needed, whether a child has one parent living or two. But expecting a child to skip adolescence in order to become a full-fledged baby-sitter, a wise household budgeter, mother's constant escort, or a steady breadwinner is overloading. And the overload may rest heavily on a burden of unresolved grief.

Agreeing with your youngsters that "Yes, it's tough to lose Dad" leaves them free to mourn. "Be brave now!" or "Be a man!" may prevent them from ventilating their grief.

Children need adults who are attentive to their feelings. They cannot identify successfully with those who are indifferent, too busy to notice, or convinced that the children have accepted the death easily. Losing a parent who had earned the living is bad enough. But losing, even temporarily, a parent who has made life *worth living* is cause for total grief in the children's world.

When a child's grief reactions are intense or prolonged, the need for special assistance is probably indicated. Contact with a family service agency can lead the parent and child to those who know how to give such help.

Mourning at Different Age Levels

Those who have studied grief in children have observed that a child experiences grief when he or she is weaned from breast or bottle, when a toy is broken, or when a beloved playmate moves to another town. While these happenings may have taught him the meaning of loss, disappointment, and minor sorrow, they are not really comparable to experiencing the death of a parent.

It is the challenging task of the surviving parent to learn how to help each child in the family, according to individual needs. *Learning* how to help is stressed, for how many parents have had training and experience to fit us for such vital action? We need help from resource persons—the family's religious counselor, the school guidance personnel, the doctor, the family service agency. Cooperation and understanding among some or all of such persons may be the key.

A few notes and observations on grief at different age levels may stimulate further learning:

The toddler. Many observers agree that the toddler has begun to understand separation, disappearance, and return. To sleep and to awaken are familiar experiences. In the game of peekaboo, the world remains, though he may hide from it, or though it may be temporarily invisible.

He knows the delight of throwing a toy away from him and having it restored to his hand. "All gone" is understood when there is no more cereal left in the bowl or in the box.

Even a two-year-old may have seen the result when a match or candle is blown out. He may have learned that trash is carried away, never to be brought back. But he has no real concept of death.

The three-to-five-year-old. To the child from three to five, awareness of death is limited. It may be partially understood as having Daddy fall asleep with the expectation of reawakening presently.

The questions asked by the child of this age will be repetitive: Where did Daddy go? When is Daddy coming home? What does die mean? Where is Daddy now?

The young child thinks concretely. The mother and any

other adults having close relationship to the child need to "take their cues" from the child, aiding him to grow in understanding at his own speed. Part of helping the child this age is to repeat the answers to the questions—simply and patiently.

The child will be inclined to look upon death as accidental and individual. He will be older before he understands that it comes to all human beings. Too much emphasis on death by accident, or death in a hospital, or death resulting from any specific cause, may generate fears of those circumstances.

When children form such an association between death and a particular position or location or condition, they need reassurance and explanation. Careful listening and observation by the parent or the nursery school teacher may reveal such need.

The five-to-ten-year-old. Children from five to ten will likely accept the death of the parent. But they may be nearing the upper end of this age grouping before they understand that death happens to everyone, and will someday happen to them. By about age ten they may see that death is final, and realize somewhat more slowly that it is also inevitable.

The school child's behavior in the classroom and on the playground may change when he is mourning. In the past, little has been attempted in the way of preparing teachers to help the child who has been bereaved. You may need to talk with your child's teacher about kinds of behavior to expect in bereavement.

A conversation between author Lynn Caine and her daughter, Buffy, shows the child's progress toward understanding death and the mother's progress in being able to handle questions. It was more than a year after her father's death when Buffy asked, "Mamma, does my daddy know I'm in first grade now?"

Uncertain how to handle the question, Lynn hesitated for a time. Finally she answered: "No, Buffy, Daddy is dead. He doesn't know you are in the first grade now. But if he did know, he'd be very pleased." And Buffy responded, "Yes, I think so.

He'd be glad I'm learning to read."[17]

The preteen. Preadolescent boys and girls may be ready to examine death's social meaning, to realize people's interdependence, and to take some share of family responsibility. But unreasoning fears and worries may still hamper their full and adequate mourning.

The adolescent. In the estimation of a number of observers, adolescent children are the most vulnerable of all when a parent's death occurs. The following short poem was written by Sara Mast, a teen-age daughter. Her family included it in a memorial booklet, printed to honor the deceased father.

MOMENTS WITH YOU

In the first quiet moments of day
A restless yearning flutters away
Like a butterfly flies.
I blink my eyes while the day is new.
What is this yearning I have for you?
Inside of my dreams, I can see
The smile that always cheered me.
For a while, I gaze at the ceiling,
Trying to choke the emotional feeling
Of losing you.[18]

Another teen-age girl I know poured out her feelings about her beloved grandfather, who had been a tireless community builder. Her thoughts were printed in the local newspaper, appropriately shared with the many people who had known him. Creative writing provides a valuable outlet for the grief of a child or youth, whether publicized or not.

A young woman who lost her father in her teens looked back from her twenty-five-year-old vantage point and wrote: "It was adolescence when my father was dying. But it's been something entirely different since the day he died." Forced prematurely into an adult role, the girl was also deprived of her father's recognition, which might have aided her in establishing identity as an adult. Normal growth processes were stopped and mourning was prevented.

A mother is so often in need of emotional companionship and support, and so concerned about protecting adolescent sons and daughters from temptations, that she constantly devises ways to hang onto teen-age children. She allows herself to become dependent upon them.

Widows' children often delay their own marriages indefinitely, especially when they have substituted in some measure for their dead fathers. Because of their commitment to helping their mothers, they may have participated less in youth activities and been slower to mature. A conscientious son may feel obligated to continue an almost matelike relationship with the mother.

If you as a widow sense such a sacrificial probability, you may decide that you must seek for yourself a satisfying single life. You may honestly want your children to have the same opportunities for education, recreation, romance, career, and homes of their own that they might have expected with two supportive parents.

Gilbert O., a man whose own college study was forsaken when his father died, came home to comfort his mother and to operate the family farm. Caught in a web of circumstance, he never returned to his studies and his earlier career plans. Years later, when his wife became terminally ill, he determined to keep history from repeating itself. He urged his teen-age son to leave for college, despite the mother's illness. He resolved to support the son's professional ambitions, however lonely he, the father, might become as a widower.

In a contrasting example, a recently widowed father I met said he planned to spend his first four retirement years by following his youngest son to the state university. The father's rationale—desiring to take courses he had been unable to include in his academic work four decades before—scarcely disguised his scheme to maintain a close relationship with the remaining adolescent child of the family.

The plan seemed fraught with problems for both father and son. Was the father unconsciously substituting the son for the dead wife and mother? Could the son have a desirable educational opportunity with the father so much in evidence? Was the father denying himself the freedom to develop his own personhood as a single individual?

Perhaps in your own shaken state you are unable to feel confidence in your adolescent children's ability to make choices. While some bereaved parents overburden their children with duties and decisions beyond their capacity, others go to the opposite extreme of interfering in the learning process for decision-making. Do you see yourself in either of these actions? Do you need to loosen the apron strings? Are you retaining enough wise and understanding parental control?

In our society, a parent's death is frequently the first death of a loved person in an adolescent's experience. The need for discussion of death is an important part of the surviving parent's role at such a time. Many new questions arise when death comes so close. And it is difficult to communicate such upsetting thoughts—especially to you, the widowed mother. Be alert for opportunities to share your thoughts, and be prepared to speak of personal feelings and convictions.

Young adult daughters and sons. Writers on children's bereavement generally cut off their books and articles short of considering the surviving parent's relationship with young adult daughters and sons. This is unfortunate, for it is the relationship which so many of us need to know about. Some or all of our children may be young adults when the father dies. We need to know their problems of accepting the death, and to discover how we may relate to them—our nearest kin.

One mother wrote of her personal agony in trying to comfort her sobbing thirty-year-old son as she told him of the surgeon's verdict, that his father was terminally ill. As the weeks and months moved on, the son struggled valiantly to aid his mother in her business tasks. He also directed the commercial enterprises in which he had been associated with his father. For mother and son to understand each other's grief was important as the schedule of duties was carried out.

Another widow observed that her young adult daughters and son acutely missed their father's occasional letters and telephone calls. Through correspondence and long-distance conversations, they had directly or indirectly sought his counsel on many matters of concern to them. Their mother realized that she would not be able to supply the very same kind of support the father had given. She wondered whether the children would confide in her, and whether she would be perceptive enough to recognize signs of major concern as her husband had done. She determined to become a better listener.

Grace T., the mother of a son in his early twenties, could not fathom his abrupt "telling her off" a few days after his father's death. Relatives had departed, and the two of them were alone for the first time since the memorial service. The mother was inexpressibly weary. Since her son Jim was unconversational much of the time, she was quite unprepared for his sudden outburst.

He was sorry his father was gone, he said, but it couldn't be helped now. "You got your jollies from being with Dad," he conceded, "but I get mine with Linda. And I'm not going to stay home because Dad died. I'm going to drive down to see Linda tonight."

His mother would have had no objection to Jim's going. After all, she and her husband approved of the romance for more than a year. Why Jim suddenly felt he must speak to her as if she might interfere with his plans mystified her. Did he think that a widowed mother was going to clutch him to her and keep him from normal youthful development? Had she shown signs of becoming dependent? Did he think he would be expected to "mother-sit"?

As she learned more about grief, Grace realized that the

lashing-out had been part of her son's mourning. Being the only person around him at the time he began to feel anger at losing his father, she naturally received the protest.

Help for Bereaved Children

You are most able to help your bereaved children when you avoid making assumptions about their grief, and become alert to feelings that have been concealed. You can learn to recognize signals for help and understanding. It is vital to the children's well-being that they be allowed and encouraged to mourn in keeping with their own feelings and levels of understanding.

To delay the children's mourning may be to hamper their development or cripple them emotionally. Children who lose a parent by death can usually carry grief work to gradual conclusion, provided they are not prevented from experiencing it as they are able.

If you take the trouble to study books and articles on explaining death to children, understanding the ways children mourn, and aiding children to mourn adequately, you will be better fitted for the complex task. Lectures and discussions on the subject may be helpful. Your religious counselor may suggest or present material concerning the child's developing concept of death.

Relating to each child as an individual with a unique approach to grief means taking time for each child. Giving the best possible care to the children may be one of your ways of expressing love for their father, now deceased.

Your bereaved children may be able to share with you in grief work and in the reorganization of life. Children can indeed "be a comfort." Their helping efforts may not be effective enough to take the place of your own physical labors. But their caring to do what they can should touch you and strengthen you for meeting new challenges.

6

You Can Grow in Widowhood

It is a significant day when you understand that life has ended for your husband, but not for you. Termination of your marriage signals the end of your interest in living only if you allow decay to set in. To realize that your life has its own uniqueness is the first step toward discovery of a new role and new objectives.

You know you are experiencing change. But you may need to be reminded that change is the common lot of all human beings, whatever our age or location.

Whether the change is in the direction of growth or decay is largely each individual's own responsibility, once the adult years have been reached. Many people live with zest for unfolding possibilities. They demonstrate that persons of thirty, fifty, seventy, and even ninety years on this earth can grow intellectually, emotionally, socially, spiritually—if only they will.

You and I cannot stay the same, no matter how much we may desire at times to maintain ourselves in a state that seems good. Whether or not we detect the changes in ourselves—many of them quite gradual—they are taking place.

But "positive change," in the form of growth and development, is by no means sure. Unless we elect to grow and develop, we change by degenerating.

We may go along for some time without understanding the difference between change and growth. Then a crisis occurs.

We are presented with circumstances for which we may be ill-prepared. "Forced off our perches," we must take a new view of ourselves and our reasons for being.

Granted, neither the woman who has had a satisfying marriage nor one whose marriage has been less than satisfying would choose widowhood as a means of gaining perspective and stimulating personal growth. Mate-loss is a crisis that strikes terrible blows to life expectations. Courage and willingness to grow are essential in the task of rebuilding.

You Can Make a New Life

Early in widowhood you do well to recognize that shifting successfully from "we" to "me" requires alterations in attitudes, habits, perspectives, and actions. Do you view choices as if you were still married? Are you acting as if your marriage must go on, despite the death of your partner? Are you continuing your life-style as it was formerly shared?

Once you grasp the concept that growth in and through widowhood is possible, you are at the point of believing that you *can* truly make a new life. You are nearing the day when you will ask yourself that momentous question, "Will the real 'me' please stand up?" You will want your true self to emerge, to become what is possible for you—first as a widowed person, and ultimately as an individual woman.

Feeling personally destroyed by great loss is common in the early weeks of widowhood. You may wonder how any building material for the new life can be salvaged. When you stand amid the debris of your world, remember that the very earth you inhabit was "created out of chaos."

Human history is rich with stories of men and women who gathered up the broken pieces, rebuilding from the ruins. Two rather famous widows exemplify such positive change.

Near the beginning of the Civil War, Annie Wittenmyer was left a well-to-do young widow with a son. Her growth, as a person concerned with the suffering of others, seems to have had roots in her private loss and in the national crisis of her time. Living in Keokuk, Iowa, the point of embarkation for most Iowa troops going south, she noted the soldiers' needs.

During the spring and summer of 1861 she wrote letters to women throughout the state, encouraging them to organize soldiers' aid societies. Such groups then sent her supplies, and money to purchase additional supplies, for distribution among the troops.

The Iowa legislature in 1862 named her one of two sanitary agents for the state. During the Battle of Shiloh she was stationed on a hospital ship. With a surgeon and two other nurses she worked around the clock, aiding the wounded. (From that battle there were 2,500 casualties among the Iowa troops alone.) Annie was also on hand at Vicksburg, caring for the wounded and supervising distribution of supplies.

Annie Wittenmyer established the first diet kitchens in army hospitals, to provide food suitable for wounded men. She organized a home for Civil War orphans at Davenport, Iowa, and became the first president of the national Women's Christian Temperance Union during her amazing personal growth in widowhood.

The second example is found in the experience of Elizabeth Ann Seton. The American wife of William Seton and mother of five children, she and her children were left living in Italy when her husband died. She was destitute in a foreign land. Aided by the Filicchi family, she was influenced by their devotion to the Roman Catholic Church. After her return to the United States, she experienced a spiritual struggle. In 1805 she was received into the Catholic Church. She opened a grade school four years later, at the invitation of Father Dubourg.

Later, when Mother Seton founded the American Sisters of Charity in Maryland, she was continuing an early concern for the sick and the poor. At one time she had been called "a Protestant Sister of Charity." During widowhood she became the first of the American Catholic school nuns. Called the "mother of the parochial school system in the United States," Elizabeth Ann Seton was canonized September 14, 1975.

Examples of change and growth during widowhood, drawn from my acquaintance, show expanded interests and creativity in the lives of several women who previously felt fulfilled as married persons. Suddenly widowed when her forty-four-year-old husband was swept away by his first-and-last heart attack, Lorna was left to finish rearing three sons alone. Ron had been an adoring husband, an outstanding father to the boys. All at once, the weight of sole responsibility for two intelligent adolescents and a third bright boy in elementary school settled on her slim shoulders.

Observers might well have expected Lorna to become an above-average single parent. But few would have supposed that she would attempt, and succeed at, building a creative new life of her own simultaneously.

Having taught high school homemaking before marriage, and having kept abreast of developments in clothing construction and fabrics, Lorna was well prepared to teach sewing classes for a time at the community college in her city. Then she sensed the potential for giving instruction in her own home, close to the junior high school her youngest son would attend.

It would be an advantage not to have to drive to evening classes. She would be in a position to determine which courses to offer, when to offer them, how many students to accept for each class. She would receive all of the tuition.

A basement room was prepared for sewing instruction. Other facilities included attractive display space where patterns, fabrics, and numerous sewing aids are sold. Lorna's mimeographed sheets of instructions and suggestions for her sewing students evolved into a printed textbook. By budgeting time wisely, Lorna gave herself wholeheartedly to the important tasks of parenting sons involved in school, church, and scout activities. She scheduled her sewing classes for the hours when the boys were at school.

Satisfying use of her education, successful business enterprise, authorship, and many worthwhile friendships resulted from Lorna's having the courage and openness to change by growing. At one point she was surprised to be building her new life without thinking how it would have been if Ron had still been with her.

When Florine N.'s dentist husband succumbed to chronic heart disease and left her alone at age fifty, Florine continued her career in public school teaching. But she also followed an urge to try something entirely new to her. To help fill the void in her life, she decided to learn to fly. A whole new world of learning opened to her when she enrolled for instruction leading to her pilot's license. Astonished friends became delighted friends when they observed Florine's perseverance and adaptability, as she progressed through her new study and flight training.

This book would never have been written if I had not been convinced that every widow has the potential for a new role in life—a role of true worth for her and for others with whom she interacts. You may have to take a voyage of self-discovery before your role is clearly seen, however.

If in widowhood you are receiving more suggestions, advice, and urgings toward specific courses of action than ever came your way before, you are in the same position as the majority of women who have recently lost their husbands. It may try both your patience and your courtesy to thank well-meaning people for their concern. You may reject or ignore much of what they say to you. Yet who on earth but you *should* be in control of your life?

Learning and practicing firmness in determining your own path into the future will help you grow and develop as "your own person." Listening well, then evaluating carefully, is part of the foundation for rebuilding in widowhood. Remembering that it is *your* life you are rebuilding is essential to independent growth. One widow remarked that "when death knocks at your door, life is there, too."

The first-year-of-bereavement studies by Glick, Weiss, and Parkes[19] indicated that over sixty percent of widows in the studies had begun to feel "like themselves" in the third month of widowhood. By that time they were at a point where new roles for them could become a reality.

Your timing of new role discovery and setting objectives may be different from that of others who have been bereaved. But prompt response to growth impulses, and the conviction that your life has worth and meaning, will move you toward the role and the objectives you adopt as your own.

Not only widows but many other persons change their careers and life-styles. We are fortunate to live in a time when more and more people realize that such change can be important for them. As you establish your new goals during widowhood, you can feel strengthened by the knowledge that others of various ages and capacities are also endeavoring to grow.

Is there a career for you? Women who already had jobs outside the home prior to loss of the husband often say that regular work has been their "salvation." They are thankful that they get tired enough to sleep at night. Perhaps the commonest advice new widows hear from those who are well into the experience is that a job or a career will help them tolerate their new status.

The new widow who has held a job is almost invariably urged to "keep right on with it." In many instances, this is reasonable advice. Yet the critical episode of widowhood may provide an unexpected opportunity to raise questions: Is this job or this career right for me? Is it the one I want to pursue now that I have single status? Is it the kind of work that best uses my talents and capacities? Is it work that brings me personal satisfaction, and also enables me to contribute something worthwhile to others' lives?

Whether you decide to seek employment for pay, to find a volunteer position, or to consider changing from the work you have been doing to some new endeavor, careful self-inventory is important. Perhaps you will benefit from consultation with a vocational counselor. A battery of vocational, interest, and psychological tests given by professional counselors for a fee may be needed. You may be able to make a good personal evaluation by listing and thinking about your own education and skills, your interests, health status, attitudes, and choice of life-style.

Your preference for indoor or outdoor work, or for day or night employment may be important considerations. Your preparation, your ability to work alone or on a team, your feelings about competition, your freedom and willingness to travel on the job, or your desire to remain close to home, may be among the factors to weigh. Women's Centers are good resource agencies for suggesting some bases for choice.

It is true that sometimes "the job chooses you," but looking at whole areas of interest before you pinpoint a certain position is a wise approach. Committing your energies in such a way that you feel part of worthwhile work may require more self-understanding than you have acquired before.

Work can provide you with "social identity and linkage with others," with self-respect, self-confidence, and increased stability. But you cannot expect to derive all these values unless the work is well chosen for you, an individual. The noted actress Helen Hayes has observed that a career is a good tranquilizer for the spirit when a woman is alone, and millions would agree. But before you settle career or job questions, ask yourself a question Helen Harris Perlman suggests, "What does your work do TO you and what does your work do FOR you?"[20]

Will your choice require further education or job training? Have you kept your yearning for learning? Are you willing to make necessary sacrifices in order to obtain the schooling or training you will need to reach new goals you have set? Assessing your financial resources, your stamina, and the degree of your commitment will surely be essential before you undertake such a program.

Chronological age need not bar you from an unusual choice. Life seemed "almost over" at age fifty-nine for Lilly Danielson Frels, a Nebraska woman, when the death of her husband "knocked the props out from under" her. For a while she "couldn't see much future."[21]

But everything changed when she decided to go back to college, in quest of the degree she had missed by dropping out to take a teaching position back in 1928. Some folks encouraged her, saying: "Go ahead. You've always wanted your degree. You'll make it."

Others warned: "Don't go. You'll find out you can't remember things like you used to. You'll study and study, but you can't keep up with the kids."

Lilly wrote a somewhat humorous account of her experiences for the Associated Press. There were plenty of hurdles to clear in carrying out her educational plans. Her transcript was long delayed. Being immunized for smallpox made her ill. She had to get new bifocal spectacles. Her skirt length dated her. She arrived on campus with her typewriter, but she had forgotten her wig. She got tired walking from building to building to confer with her future instructors.

Yet she had some advantages. She lived in a quiet wing of the dormitory. The only boys on her mind were sons and grandsons. No dates cut in on her study hours. She was older than most of her teachers, but more motivated to learn than many of the younger students.

Her grown-up family proved supportive of her educational ambitions. One son even kidded her when she left for college, "We'll get a report if you get a down slip, won't we?"

Lilly succeeded in fulfilling present degree requirements—forty-eight hours of course work. With her Bachelor of Science in vocational home economics and secondary education in hand, she felt that whether or not she found any market for brand-new college grads in their sixties, she was definitely "living again, not rusting"!

Commanding Your Hours

Whether you choose to work outside the home or to pursue interests that can be developed chiefly in your own residence, you may need to learn to command your hours. You may have had time on your hands early in widowhood, only to discover that you have gradually allowed others to fill your hours for you. Or you may find that you have misjudged the amount of time some activities would consume. Insufficient time is left for that which you really desire to accomplish.

How sad if your work is simply a drug to make you forget for eight hours a day that you have been bereaved! How tragic if you do a job to escape reality! How depressing if you work without any sense of mission in life, without caring!

The decision to make your time count is a key decision for growth in your present and future. A job can help structure your time. But it needs to be a job that has meaning for you, if you are to grow.

Devoting some time and energy to creative urges is important to people at any age, and often doubly significant to those who have been widowed. One widow correspondent wrote that she "learned not to expect the excitement and joy" she had known in the past. Yet she found herself launching into new, thrilling experiences. She was using her blocks of alone time for following artistic urges she had long suppressed. As her creativity increased, she did away with many "waste motions," in order to free still more hours for her chosen projects.

Your single-parent family cares may seem so heavy that you tend to reject any thought of claiming time for your own development. Do you feel guilty about leaving the children in others' care, yet long to have adult experiences?

Joyce B., a widow with two small youngsters, told me she no longer feels uncomfortable about being away from the children at times, in the interest of her own growth. "I think I am a better mother for having been away—sometimes attending a church convention several days—than I would be if I never left my children. I am particular about their care, and I spend much time with them myself. But when I satisfy my own needs for intellectual and social stimulation and expression, I come back a more fulfilled person, a better parent."

Edna R., a somewhat older widow, confided recognition of her needs as a person and how she had asserted herself effectively: "My teen-age daughter informed me the other night that she was going out on a date. It was nearly six P.M., and I had a nice supper on the table. I was left to eat alone.

"I got to thinking of several times I had turned down invitations from women friends because I felt I must get my daughter's meals. The next time I was asked out, I accepted. My daughter was home that evening.

" 'What am I going to do?' she asked. 'There is plenty in the refrigerator for you to get yourself some supper,' I told her. 'The other night you went on a date on very short notice, and I was left to eat alone. Tonight I have an invitation out. I think I need to get out, just as you do.' "

Arlene K., who had never traveled alone anywhere, feared her children might become sick in her absence if she went on a vacation without them. "What would others think of me, leaving the kids? And what if the money I spend is needed later for some emergency?"

Yet she and her husband had sometimes left the children behind while the two of them vacationed. Should it be different because she was now solely responsible? Finally she decided for the trip alone. "After all," she concluded, "I am a person, too. I need time to myself and interests of my own."

Reviewing the experience later on, she commented: "It was the best decision I made last year. I have accepted the idea that

I am alone. I do what I want to do. No matter what we do, there is always someone who is going to think we're not doing the right thing. No one is going to keep my life going if I don't."

A father who is also a single parent put it this way, "I love the kids, but they're not enough." And a wise counselor added, "You won't be a single parent with kids at home forever."

Think about yourself as a role model for your children. Will they benefit more from emulating a mother who martyrs herself by spending all her time and energy on caring for them, or from patterning after a mother who strikes a good balance between child care and other personally rewarding activity in her life?

If you think you are going to be too heavily burdened to attempt an activity just because it appeals to you, you may be inspired by reading of a creative widow who could easily have put aside all artistic urges in favor of family cares. Jo Widner's story appeared in *Sioux City Magazine* on February 18, 1976. Nine years before, she had been widowed and left with fourteen children. What could she possibly do but devote herself to caring for her large family? How could a widow with such unusual responsibility take any time off for the development of her creative interests?

Jo's older children were the ones who suggested that their bereaved mother take classes at the Art Center, develop her long-neglected talent, and find interests outside the home. They even chauffered her to the Art Center the first time she attended classes there.

Eventually Jo joined the Sioux City Artists' Group. She agreed to share a studio with another artist, working there in the afternoons. She commented: "A strong interest like this is important for a woman my age. At some point the kids will be gone and then she needs something of her own. When I paint, I'm in my own world. I can forget everything. It's good therapy."

Specializing in portraits, Jo does some commissioned work to help supplement her income. Many of the portraits are in oil, but she also works fairs in the summer, doing charcoal and pastel portraits. As she puts it, "Painting is a joy for me, especially the pieces of work I do for myself—the ones that grow out of my own ideas."

Only You Can Be You

Knowing that you cannot help changing, will you settle for a merely livable life in widowhood, or will you foster your own personal growth? Will you be just able to "get along somehow," or will you build strength and renew vigor as you discover what is possible for you in this period of your life? Will you remain passive, letting opportunities go by? Or will you become active in promoting your own development as a person?

A widow wrote in the *THEOS Newsletter* that a banner she once saw at a Marriage Encounter workshop came to her mind in widowhood. It read: "God Doesn't Make Junk." She said the banner reminded her "that God did make me capable of being my own person; a person with my own special values, talents, and free will to make decisions. I knew then that I could develop my own interests; that I could be a more confident 'Mary.' ME!"[22]

However crushed you may have felt at the view society takes of widows, you can draw strength and confidence from the theological valuing of persons. As an anonymous poet put it, "in the mind of God, I am unique and irreplaceable." No one else can be you! And you can grow now, just as you have grown in other stages of your life.

Study yourself. Take a penetrating look at careers and avenues of expression, observing how others have been able to grow and develop as worthy persons. Determine how to stimulate your own purposeful change. You may find help in reading, attending lectures, availing yourself of various kinds of counseling, and perhaps enrolling for classes in the fields of your interest.

To learn some of the values and the special techniques of living alone graciously, what more logical instructors can widows turn to than to women who have elected to be single for the sake of a self-giving career, who live by themselves in preference to marrying unwisely, or who live singly because there is an imbalance between the numbers of marriageable men and women in our society?

Among the values people see in single living are: (1) the chance to grow personally and enrich oneself culturally; (2) the greater mobility, permitting more travel; (3) the opportunity for more individual decisions, without consultation unless one wishes it; (4) career choice, minus encumbrances; (5) freedom for public service, paid or unpaid; (6) less distraction if you want to paint, write, perform musically, do research, or pursue any goal requiring deep concentration; (7) fulfillment through learning to live not only usefully but vibrantly.

New behavior may be required in order to grow. You may have to develop inner resources that have lain dormant. You may have to experience a kind of spiritual renaissance, to be able to progress in the direction you choose. Some observers may think you are becoming a different person. You may realize that you are becoming more yourself!

Whatever that new role, those who have grown in widowhood generally agree that it must be significant—something that "gets you up in the morning" with anticipation and purpose. It must generate the kind of enthusiasm that makes you reach out expectantly to the future, to your new womanhood.

7

Managing Your Money

Most of us are confused and bewildered when we first face the sole responsibility for family finances. It is a common plight not to know where one stands in the matter of income and resources, especially at the beginning. No wonder widows are advised to postpone decisions until they have taken inventory, familiarized themselves with the possibilities, and selected their own advisory "teams"!

First realize that money or its lack will control you, unless you learn to control it. Then you are ready to begin assessing a new financial situation and developing skills for conducting your living arrangements. If you never have understood business matters, you can learn now.

Progress from panic to eventual order and composure can be predicted if you are willing to avail yourself of many aids to better understanding and prudent planning. If you had little to do with family business affairs in the past, it will take some time to acquire the know-how. But bankers, lawyers, brokers, and others in the business world point out that when women rid themselves of the idea that they cannot understand money matters, they often become good budgeters, good planners, and good investors.

More than that, women constantly are proving themselves capable of supporting their families, managing their households alone, selling or buying property, comprehending and even computing their taxes, making and living with their own decisions. Women, including widows, can become skilled problem solvers.

Those who have already held jobs in business, or who have had experience in keeping books for their households will be better prepared for financial roles in widowhood. But even the woman who has never needed nor wanted to put her mind to business matters can develop the desired skills for handling them well.

Go early to impartial sources of help. Women's Centers, Family Services, or university extension staffs can supply reliable guidelines. Delay can be costly in terms of cash, unnecessary worry, and inconvenience. No time should be lost in selecting and consulting your own "panel" of financial and legal advisers. Seeking and finding sound advice to govern the financial program you develop for yourself is basic.

Immediate Concerns

You may feel inept at first, and unsure that you want to be in charge of your finances. You will probably fare much better if you do the managing rather than delegate it to another. Why not make up your mind to manage knowledgeably and efficiently?

You don't have to flounder about where you stand financially for long. You can begin your inventory almost immediately, taking stock of assets that spring to mind, and completing the list as you sort through whatever records you and your husband kept. You must determine as soon as possible exactly what income, savings, and property are yours to be concerned with.

All possible benefits from insurance policies (be sure to check special provisions!), pension funds, social security, Veterans' Administration, fraternal organizations, and other sources should be checked out promptly. Widows are often surprised to discover sources they had forgotten, or had not paid close attention to, when the protection was purchased.

Laverne T., a widow whose husband was killed in a bus accident, was well aware of her husband's several life insurance policies. But she was surprised to learn that a disability policy he carried provided a large benefit in the event of death in a passenger car, or in several types of public transportation. The unexpected benefit helped her to pay in full some of her husband's obligations which had worried her greatly. How relieved she was—and how impressed with this extra evidence of her husband's care of her!

To which benefits are you entitled? Have you applied for your husband's death benefits from social security? If you are under sixty and caring for the child or children of your husband, who was a worker covered under social security, you will be eligible to receive payments until the youngest child is eighteen. Have you a child or children under twenty-two studying full time in a college or other educational institution? These children are entitled to payment also. Are you past sixty, or past fifty and disabled? In either case, you are eligible for payment. A visit to the nearest social security office will provide you with needed information, and necessary application forms.

Was your husband a veteran of military service? Contact the Veterans' Administration for any burial benefit or educational benefits for which you or your children might be eligible.

Did your husband belong to a burial association or other group providing benefits you should claim? You can list and promptly notify the insurance companies with whom your husband was insured. Claim forms may have to be filled out in order to collect. You may want to discuss with your advisers whether to take full payment immediately or elect to receive payments over a longer period. Not only your needs but also the potential return on various kinds of savings and investments will have to be determined before you can make such a decision wisely.

One widow wrote me that in her experience it had been

reassuring to have the assistance of the same attorney, banker, doctor, and auto mechanic who had formerly aided her husband in the home community. She was well pleased with the advice given in response to her early widowhood inquiries, and confident that she could trust these persons for the foreseeable future.

Finding a Good Attorney

But you may have been left to head your family without knowing legal or business advisers you can depend upon. Where can you turn? How can you locate and establish yourself with the professional persons qualified to guide you in determining your new financial course?

If you have not previously consulted a lawyer, or are dissatisfied for good reason with the one you and your husband dealt with, one of your first requirements will surely be to choose your legal adviser. A financial consultant once advised a farmer trying to find a good lawyer to do three things:

1. Ask several of the most successful persons you know who their lawyers are.
2. Discuss estate planning with a bank trust officer, and ask him to recommend two or three good lawyers.
3. Visit with the recommended attorneys to talk over the services you think you will need. Learn the probable costs. Find out whether your personalities are sufficiently compatible. If there is a charge for a brief visit of this kind, it should be small.

You might also do well to inquire of several other widows where they have obtained dependable, reasonably priced legal advice. It is sensible to get an estimate of how much the work of settling your husband's estate will cost. Good attorneys expect to make such estimates. An attorney doesn't get paid more because an estate takes longer to settle. It is sometimes quite advantageous to leave the estate open for a period of time.

Remember that cost is not the only criterion in choosing your lawyer. You want an attorney who is accurate, and experienced enough to advise you well. In some communities, the local bar association or legal aid society may be of some assistance. However, the bar association's lawyer referral service is only that, not an endorsement. It simply says, "Here are three qualified lawyers." You have to make the choice.

What a help it will be if you are able to find a satisfactory lawyer not many miles away! If you must travel far—all the more reason to "get your head together" before each trip, preparing carefully the questions you need to have answered at each point in time.

Your attorney knows you have fears and worries. None will sound childish or silly to him or her. Your lawyer will probably be quite willing to have you use him as a kind of whipping boy in your business contacts. In resisting pressures to make investments or changes in savings arrangements, you can say, "I will talk with my attorney." He will probably counsel you not to make quickly any decisions that substantially change your way of living or way of doing business.

One widow was pressed by a good friend, who had written her husband's chief life insurance policies, to "buy some more protection." Since she had insurance to cover her own last expenses, and her children were grown and educated, she wondered how the life insurance he was suggesting could protect her. Her funds would draw considerably higher interest if placed in insured certificates of deposit or sound investments.

It has been suggested that there ought to be a law invalidating all business transactions made by a widow for six months after the husband's death—unless cosigned by her lawyer! The time of mingled grief and early experimentation in a new role is a period when safeguards are badly needed. Some widows take a father, brother-in-law, or trusted friend to accompany them when they buy a car, a house, or a large appliance. They feel that such support strengthens their resolution not to be influenced by high-pressure sales tactics.

Selecting a Reliable Bank

A reliable bank is important for you as a widow. You may be well satisfied to continue with the same institution you and your husband used as a couple. But your ease of transportation to and from the bank, the degree of trust felt toward the bank's personnel, your confidence in the particular bank's methods of making transactions, and general satisfaction with the services available through the bank should be considered.

In some instances, keeping savings and checking accounts in more than one bank may be desirable. For example, you may live in an area where you are very well known. You may want greater privacy for some of your business. If you have more funds than can be insured in one bank, you may seek an additional location for insured savings. If he is told your intention, your family banker may offer to assist in the transfer of some savings to another bank he recommends. Care should be taken to inform trusted relatives that you have deposits in more than one bank.

Personalized help with financial planning is rapidly becoming part of modern banking service. A special counselor for widows is on the staff of some banks. A number of banks now advertise "Plan Ahead" centers to aid customers with their problems. Choice of a bank may hinge upon the kind of service offered, other factors being equal.

If you inherited a large estate, you may be in need of an investment manager. Be prepared to pay an annual fee—on top of whatever brokerage fees are involved—to have a professional management firm take over your investment decisions. Your goals (current income, long-term growth, safety), the firm's credentials and performance records, and the fees should be examined before you choose the firm. Investment managers who urge the widow to "hurry and sign up" are usually not with the reputable firms. Take your time!

Rather than pay an investment manager and delegate the

investment decisions, many widows prefer to learn to invest their own funds. In the section on investments in this chapter, suggestions for such involvement are offered.

The insurance agent you need as a widow may or may not be the same individual who served your husband. Your situation is greatly altered with respect to life insurance. Your age and insurability, the age and status of your children, and your chief occupation will have to be taken into account. As you weigh the costs and values of various plans, you will surely want a trusted insurance representative to explain the possibilities. You will be well advised to talk over the proposals with several impartial advisers before any decisions are made.

Record-Keeping

Within days of your bereavement you probably realized the importance of keeping good financial records and having them filed in an efficient manner. This was true for me. I received notice shortly after my husband's death, in a letter addressed to him, that there was no record of payment for a load of ground corncobs delivered some weeks earlier. Could proof of such payment be supplied to the seller?

I consulted the farm ledger, learned the number of the canceled check, and soon mailed a photocopy of the check to the man who had inquired. How relieved I felt that there was no question that the bill had been paid! And how determined I was to continue to keep accurate records I might need at various times in the future.

A university instructor who teaches single parents how to manage their finances insists that they run all money received through the checking account, and draw all money out by check, as bills are paid. She feels that a checking account is a necessity for keeping track of income and expenditure—the most valuable record-keeping tool.

When you write a check, she advises, it takes only seconds

to fill in—first on the stub, and then on the face of the check —enough specific information to identify the category of the expenditure. Use the "for" blank! You should write the date to which a subscription, or an insurance premium, is being paid by the check. Add the phrase "in full" or "through date" when settling a bill for charges that have been made over a period of time. It is wise to avoid making the check for more than the amount of the bill. The value of the check as a record is decreased if made for the purchase plus cash.

Looking up a payment record in your checkbook is quicker than going through a whole stack of checks. Once you have noted the check number, it is easy to locate the check—providing you have placed them all in sequence at the end of each year.

To keep a balanced checkbook, an accurate account of expenditures, and to be able to determine easily the monthly and yearly totals in various categories, you will likely decide that a small calculator is an essential piece of your home office equipment. Its portability makes it useful—even for checking costs per pound when shopping for groceries.

The way you organize your home "office"—whether it is a room, or a desk in a corner—is basic to your record-keeping, and probably to the orderly conduct of your financial affairs. Strive to develop your own personal system, one that works for you. Whether you use a regular office file or a packing box to hold those file folders, manila envelopes, or expansible paper portfolios from the stationery store, the important thing is that your records are logically labeled and placed so that you have them at your fingertips!

Most of us carry our driver's license, social security card, auto insurance card, hospital insurance card, credit cards, and information on any specific diseases or allergies to drugs, with us in our billfolds. Birth certificates, military records, church records, marriage and divorce documents, auto titles, bills of sale, bonds, and stock certificates belong in the bank safe-deposit box. That is also the place to keep employment information, mortgages, contracts, debt notes, the signed will or a copy of the will, the passport, the abstracts for property owned, and the household inventory. Snapshots of your home's rooms, showing major furnishings, will make that household inventory easier.

Account books, bank passbooks, bank statements, deposit slips, check stubs, canceled checks, and receipts should be kept in a current file in your home office. There you should also have insurance policies of all kinds, medical records, mortgage amortization records, numbers of credit cards with the firms' addresses, a list of papers kept in your safe-deposit box, and a copy of that household inventory.

Filed at home you may have important canceled checks (for real estate, large purchases, taxes, securities purchased, and rent), guarantees and warranties, tax records, educational records, receipts to support tax deductions, records of major improvements to the house, and documents pertaining to real estate ownership.

If you are like me, you need to learn what to toss! You may have lacked the courage to throw away canceled checks of small or routine amounts, payroll check stubs (the yearly withholding statement has the necessary information), and routine bills (only the latest one is needed to show the balance after previous payment). Check on your particular state's limit for filing suit (usually from two to six years), and dispose of all space takers that are no longer needed.

Settling Your Husband's Estate

My attorney gave me a few simple instructions to govern record-keeping during the expected eighteen-month period of settling my husband's estate. Estate expenses would include: (1) anything that would have been part of the farm account, (2) any expense—personal, household, farm—prior to the date of my husband's death, and (3) any funeral or burial expense.

The federal inheritance tax would be due in fifteen months, he advised; the state inheritance tax would be due in eighteen months. (New legislation has reduced these times.) He advised me to place any available funds in insured savings until those dates, thus earning interest as long as possible before payment had to be made.

In general, you will be well advised to keep your affairs private. Letting all the relatives and neighbors know the size of insurance benefits, savings, and other resources invites much unsolicited advice and gossip. You will do better to confide in only two or three discreet individuals who prove themselves good sounding boards for discussion of finances.

Withholding information about your financial affairs from prying salesmen who telephone or come to your door may seem such an elementary means of protection that it need not be mentioned. Yet many widows, lonely for someone to talk with, and lacking confidence regarding business matters, are easily drawn into chatting with such persons. Facts better kept private may be revealed. Simply state that you are not interested in discussing certain matters, or in answering questions. This will come quite naturally after you think a little in advance about firm but courteous replies you can give.

Pressures from adult children to borrow from you may have to be resisted. A widow owes it to herself and to society to retain her own financial security if possible. A depression or a lengthy illness may overtake you and deplete your funds. Gifts of money or property can seldom be reclaimed if they are needed. Some senior citizens observe that adult children are more considerate, more attentive, if the parent's income and resources are a partial mystery!

Despite such warnings, you may still feel that you are in a good position to lend a thousand dollars or so to a son or daughter getting started, and needing more to buy a car or make a down payment on a house. You better raise some questions! Is the loan the best way to develop self-reliance in the young person? If you do lend the money, is your son or daughter willing to sign a note and place it in your safe-deposit box? Is this money you can actually spare if it is not returned on schedule? Have you consulted your trusted advisers about the wisdom of making the loan? Would you expect the amount to be deducted from the borrower's share of your estate, should you die before it is repaid? If so, consult your attorney concerning legal arrangements that may be necessary.

The very mention of possible sale of your property, some of your household goods, your husband's farm machinery, his boat or hunting gear, may trigger negative feelings at first. But when you consider how each item is to be used, housed, and maintained as part of your changing life pattern, you may gradually discover that a sale of some kind *is* indicated.

I well remember how sure I was in those first weeks of widowhood that no auction sale of my husband's farm machinery would be needed. Naively I thought that well-placed ads offering a few items to be sold privately would take care of the matter. After advertising and quickly selling a new sprayer for its approximate cost, I was all the more convinced that my assumption was correct.

What I did not take into account was the total amount of equipment in scattered locations on the premises. To dispose of it a little at a time, with a succession of buyers telephoning and coming to see the different items, would take months! Besides, as a sensible neighbor pointed out, there would be many small tools and supplies, many salvageable materials, still not cleaned up after the large machinery was finally sold.

Gradually the light dawned. An auction sale of machinery, our large herd, and all the miscellany collected in twenty years of farming *was* actually the best way to convert those assets into money. The proceeds could be placed in insured savings. At the same time, the farmstead would be tidied and prepared for a prospective cash renter.

Garage sales, which have become so common, are the choice

of many people who have a comparatively small number of household items they wish to sell. But garage sales have their pitfalls, as those who have had articles walk away undetected or seen checks bounce could attest. Better wise up before you plan such a sale! Have some watchers to aid you. If you have a large quantity of valuable furniture and appliances you wish to sell, it may pay you to deal instead with a good auctioneer.

Selling real estate or a business is likely to be of such major concern that you should postpone it until you have studied the situation with several impartial advisers. Give yourself time to think, time to regain your full physical and mental strength. Hurried decisions in this area could be disastrous.

We cannot always expect to profit from disposing of possessions that have been prized. About a year after her husband's death, Evelyn H. had not made any disposition of the ham radio equipment he had long enjoyed. After a number of inquiries into its current value, she learned that much of the equipment was obsolete, or impractical to move. She accepted a nominal amount from a hobbyist who was willing to take it all. Evelyn felt that some things would now be used by one who had an interest similar to her husband's, and that the rest would be off the premises. She would have additional room for her own hobbies.

Your Long-Range Financial Planning

Your long-range financial plans should probably wait until you learn just what income you can count on. You need to know the full extent of your benefits and resources, and the projected expenditures necessary for your life-style as a single person, or as a single-parent family.

When you have kept careful accounts for a year, you will know much better what the groceries, utilities, car maintenance, health insurance, repairs, and housekeeping supplies may amount to, in your present circumstances. You will then be ready to budget for your various needs.

Statistics are sometimes cited to show that the majority of widows spend all of the husband's insurance during the first year after his death. This may happen when the amount of insurance carried is really inadequate. But often it occurs because the widow simply does not realize that she is living too extravagantly. Living beyond income, and being also a victim of inflation, one can soon be deeply in debt.

If you and one or more of your children are drawing social security benefits, you should be aware that your own benefit will end when you no longer have a child under age eighteen, not to resume until you are age sixty, or disabled. You should also bear in mind that the educational benefit for unmarried children who are full-time students ends at age twenty-two. The "widow's gap" between the time when the youngest child reaches eighteen and the time when the mother turns sixty is important in long-range planning.

For most women, widowhood means less financial support than they have been used to. Though the husband might have drawn a pension eventually, that plan probably ended with his death. And when the widow becomes eligible for social security, she may draw much less at age sixty than her husband would have drawn at age sixty-five. Much of the husband's life insurance may go to pay the unexpected expenses of final illness. No wonder employment outside the home is so often urgent for the middle-aged, as well as the younger, widow!

You may have to become a real student of ways to economize. You can learn to compare as you shop, to be deliberate rather than impulsive in buying, to investigate thoroughly before you buy.

Having to shift down in spending is harder than shifting up. But you will have lots of company as you strive to line up income and expenses evenly.

Developing a budget is a vital step in long-range planning. Both a monthly and a yearly budget help guide your spending and your saving. You will be better able to control your funds, once you have set this down on paper. When you look ahead and list the months of the year, noting when to expect certain large expenses, you can avoid being caught unprepared. Likewise, when you work toward, and achieve, financial goals you have set, you know you are growing in self-reliance.

Many excellent budget guides are available from various sources to help you categorize your projected expenditures. But the chances are that not one will be perfect for your needs. Until you decide what your categories are, you may be glad to have a printed guide, and to be aware what percentages of income are suggested for housing, food, transportation, recreation, etc. Eventually you may find that you are better able to make the determination than any "expert."

How does widow status affect your credit rating? Adversely, if you have never established a credit record of your own, separate from your husband's. In a small, rural community, people who knew you and your husband as a financially reliable couple will trust you. But outside the community you will likely find it necessary to build your record from scratch. Granted, this is unfair, considering that you shared bills and payments with your husband. But if only his name was used, you will probably have to establish your own record.

In the event that your husband did not have a good credit rating, your task may be much harder. Applying for a small loan from your bank or credit union, and repaying it readily, gets your loan and payments "on the record." A purchase on the installment plan, and payment with your personal check, helps establish you as a good credit risk. If credit at a department store is desired, one can request a modest line, and show proof that one has paid a telephone or electric bill promptly.

In *Sylvia Porter's Money Book,*[23] rules are suggested for use of credit cards. Credit cards are for those who have steady income, a habit of paying promptly, and stable rather than impulsive buying habits.

To use credit cards to your best advantage:

1. Accept only those cards you actually need and will use regularly. For most, one bank charge card and maybe a couple of oil company cards for gas are enough.

2. Treat every purchase you are planning to charge as you would a cash purchase. Ask yourself whether you really want and need the item. Can you really afford it?

3. At the beginning of each month, decide on a maximum total of charges you'll be able to repay easily. Stick within that limit, and repay the charges promptly to avoid finance charges.

4. Keep all your receipts until you receive your statement to check your spending and your totals against the statement for errors.

To protect yourself:

5. Go over every card you own. Make sure you have destroyed all you do not need. Cut unwanted cards in half and throw them away.

6. Make a list of all credit cards you decide to keep with the names and addresses of the issuers and the account numbers. Keep this list in a safe place, but *not* in your wallet.

7. Sign each new card you decide to keep. This will force anyone trying to use the card fraudulently to forge your signature—a definite deterrent to the amateur.

8. Check your credit card collection every two or three weeks. If any card is missing, inform the issuer immediately—first by phone, then by letter or telegram in which you refer to your call.

9. Never lend your card to anyone.

10. Make sure your card is returned to you each time you use it. Among the major suppliers of credit cards to fraudulent users are dishonest employees of legitimate establishments.

What if you have been refused credit but do not understand why? You can review your credit file, upon request and after presentation of proper identification to the consumer reporting agency which has issued a credit report about you. Most local credit bureaus are members of Associated Credit Bureaus, Inc., 6767 Southwest Freeway, Houston, Tex. 77036. They are glad to answer questions you have about your credit record or your rights under the Fair Credit Reporting Act.

A woman widowed two months, and without any experience in managing money, wrote that she was delighted to find a planning center in her bank. A counselor "put all the pieces of her financial mess together" and set up a complete program of what she should do, including retirement provision and a monthly budget. But many do not have access to such planning centers. And most of us will gain confidence if we ourselves conduct our financial affairs.

An investment counselor may be needed by the widow with considerable wealth. A farm management service may make sense for the woman who inherits a great deal of land. But the charges for such assistance are high. Whatever is decided, it is a growing experience for most widows to discipline themselves to be well informed about money matters affecting them.

Keeping a Fiscal Calendar

As soon as you can, begin to keep your own calendar of fiscal responsibility so that you know what you must do and when. Remember to renew your driver's license and to buy the annual auto license, and renew your auto insurance. Having your car serviced regularly will not likely be neglected if you have written reminders to yourself. Your annual or semiannual medical examination will be carried out if you schedule it well in advance—perhaps during the week of your birthday.

Will you be paying quarterly on your estimated income tax? Better sit right down and post the times when payments are due to the Internal Revenue Service and the state treasurer! Is there a life insurance premium due annually? Having the due date for all insurance premiums on the calendar will help you to be prepared.

Speaking of insurance, have you updated your household inventory since you became a widow? Is the amount of insurance realistic? In case of a fire, tornado, or robbery, have you a list and/or snapshots of each room's furnishings in your safe-deposit box?

You need to know where you stand with regard to each appropriate type of insurance for your new circumstances. Is your dwelling adequately covered? Is your homeowners coverage adequate for your new situation? Is your liability to others in case of an auto accident sufficient?

In the first months of my widowhood, with my thoughts still somewhat disorganized, I paid unquestioningly several policies protecting farm buildings or equipment. I had neither the strength nor the inclination to study each policy then. I simply trusted my late husband's judgment, and kept them all in force. The following year, as premium notices arrived, I took the trouble to study them. With dismay, I discovered that I had paid the previous fall to insure a tractor that had been sold.

Some widows have said that managing money is often more difficult than earning it! Studying finances and keeping accounts may never have been your bag. You may have to sweat and strain to become informed. You may have to weather some foolish mistakes. But you can train yourself to conduct your financial affairs acceptably. Yes, you can!

Savings and Investments

What to do about savings, investments, and indebtedness will be among your important concerns. If you are uninformed in this area, try to read on these subjects *before* you discuss the possibilities with selected advisers. What they have to say won't mean much unless you have familiarized yourself with the vocabulary, at least. Learning the lingo of savings and investments will make you more knowledgeable and confident.

Specific goals for your savings—money for your child's education, for a trip abroad, for retirement—can motivate you to decide what amount you will deposit from each paycheck. If you have $10,000 or more to invest, inquire about the annual returns on U.S. Government bills, notes, and bonds, or federal agency securities. An alert banker can inform you. When the rate is favorable, you can earn very well for six months, a year, or eighteen months—and have the return in hand when it is time to pay inheritance taxes.

If the rate is no longer favorable at the end of the period, the principal can be placed in a certificate of deposit at the bank or savings and loan. Ask how much your bank charges for the transaction before you make a purchase of U.S. Government bills, notes, bonds, etc. There is considerable variation.

Probably you already know that you should have sufficient money set aside for medical and other emergencies before you purchase stocks. If you really want to place some funds in stocks, but shrink from active participation, you may be a prime candidate for mutual funds, so-called. But you should know that there is no guarantee that these funds will prosper, any more than that stocks you select will rise in value.

How about those tax-exempt municipal bonds? Financial writers often refer to them as a "tricky affair" for which a widow needs expert, professional investment advice. Sometimes the high interest rates and tax-exempt status of municipal bonds is played up, but the investor is hardly aware of the longer period (perhaps twelve years) during which the money is committed. As for serious investing in diamonds, silver, rare books, antiques, or art masterpieces—such dealings are for the highly knowledgeable, not for the novice collector.

Your Stewardship

The whole concept of stewardship is due for review in widowhood. Indications are that thoughtful stewardship may be more common among the poor and just-adequate income groups than among the well-to-do. In our affluent society many women inherit large estates. If you are one of these, you know that you are a woman of means, but for a year or so you may be uncertain what your expenditures will be in your new life alone. How will you be able to determine the extent of your giving, at the same time retaining enough to secure your living in old age?

Probably more widows give stingily than contribute their "very living," as did the giver of the Biblical widow's mite. You may be afraid that you will not have enough left to keep you from becoming dependent if you give generously. You may need help in budgeting your contributions to church, charities, health drives, and miscellaneous appeals. Learn how to do long-range planning in the area of stewardship. Some church denominations, private colleges, and charitable institutions stand ready to present plans for those willing to designate a gift of money or property, with assurance of lifetime income.

If you have children to rear, you may think you cannot afford to give anything because you need every cent to make ends meet. Do you want your children to gather the impression that giving is only for those who have plenty? However small the gifts must be, stewardship has to be practiced if it is to be learned.

At the same time, widows especially need to be on guard against the many religious con games and salvation rackets that are run for the benefit of the promoters. Just when you are emotionally vulnerable, someone may try to persuade you to sign away money or property. Religious projects can sound very appealing. Whenever such appeals pressure you to give without delay, it is wise to wait and to investigate.

8

Other Decisions You Must Make

A good maxim to follow in regard to decision-making is "Think now; sign later." When you are pressured to hurry a decision, you can resolve to go through orderly steps of problem-solving before you choose your route. You can offer the explanation that "my attorney wants me to wait," whenever you need to slow down.

Postpone most of the important decisions until you feel composed and well-informed. You will be wise to make lists and assign priorities on a daily, weekly, and monthly basis. Such listing will assure consideration of important matters within sufficient time. It will also help you to table some concerns while you give attention to more urgent matters.

From personal experience I know that some quite important decisions may have to be dealt with before you are at all ready for them. You may need a new way of thinking through problems for yourself. You can develop a kind of rational thinking that is applicable to the various problems you now face and will face. It will pay to "take the deep breath" and look at the steps in problem-solving before you work through to any further solutions. Learning and practicing these steps may slow you down temporarily. But in the end, you will be "running much faster" if you observe the following steps in problem-solving:[24]

1. Make a preliminary statement of the problem. State the problem clearly and concisely to get it into focus. State also

what you think is causing the problem. If you face many problems, state several of them, assign priorities.

2. Select one problem to zero in on. As soon as the choice is made, begin to collect needed information concerning the matter. Continue until you are reasonably satisfied that you have the pertinent facts.

3. Analyze information. By studying the information gathered, you can determine what more is needed. You can move toward a solution by a process of reasoning, once you know the givens.

4. Develop a plan. To arrive at the best plan, it is often necessary to state several alternate plans. The implications of each should be considered—the involvement of money and energy; the possible spin-offs. What exactly is your goal in the matter? How are you going to reach it?

Your choice of the final plan for solving a specific problem may prove to be a synthesis of several of the alternate plans you have developed and stated.

Your Decisions

One of your decisions will surely be about your work. If you have devoted your chief energies to homemaking while your husband was living, are you content to go on in that pursuit now? Do you need to earn? Do you desire the stimulation of a part-time or full-time job that interests you and brings you into contact with people? Do you know the possibilities for volunteer work in your city or rural area?

Here is an opportunity to apply the method of problem-solving just outlined. The problem may be to decide what "your kind" of work really is. Gathering information may take several months and some journeying about. List-making, reading, and thinking before you set out may save time and gasoline. Counseling available through a Women's Center or an employment service may help you to decide about the work you prefer.

Analysis of the information you gather might well be charted in a simple way, so that you can compare the attractions, the rewards, the disadvantages, and the suitability of the types of work you have been investigating. Finding work that you believe you can perform creditably, and even joyfully, may be far better than settling for a well-paying but stifling position.

You may have management skills you elect to use in running the farm (perhaps with the help of teen-age sons and daughters) or other business. Know-how gained from working with your husband, and strong motivation to keep a business or a farm in the family, can combine to spur such challenging work. You have to be the judge as to whether you have the enthusiasm and the vitality for a vocation of this kind.

If you want to explore employment possibilities, there are many sources. Nearly all of the popular women's magazines have listings and articles that may stimulate your thinking. So do publications such as the American Association of University Women's *Journal*. Your local library may have references such as *Catalyst*, a series of booklets on career opportunities, or *New Job Opportunities for Women*, by Muriel Lederer and the Editors of *Consumer Guide* (Simon & Schuster, Inc., 1975). Another book on the subject is *The Women's Work Book*, by Karen Abarbanel and Gonnie Siegel (Praeger Publishers, Inc., 1975).

Job advice, employment projections, and statistics may be obtained from the Women's Bureau, Employment Standards Administration, U.S. Department of Labor, Washington, D.C. 20210. You may make interesting discoveries when you inquire locally, at the nearest state employment service office.

Another decision may involve your residence. The appropriateness, comfort, and convenience of your dwelling for the life you will now live need to be evaluated. Whether you like the home you have shared in the past and want to stay in it is a prime consideration. So is your financial capacity to maintain it in good condition.

Widows who have written to me have indicated that the

decision about residence often says more about the state of the emotions than one might at first realize: "There is no perfect place. . . . Mine was a gradual decision and a change. . . . I had security in owning my house. . . . It was a decision to pray about. . . . Don't go home with family or friends. Stay in your home until you find out what you want. . . . You can't run away. . . . I tell other widows, 'Keep your home.' . . . A trip several months after Joe died gave me time to think out what I would do about my residence."

You will surely want to list your own criteria for your dwelling. As a widow you will want to confirm your choice on the basis of the life-style that is emerging for you. Your work, your entertaining, your hobbying, and your taste in architecture can all enter into the decision. Remember to check the neighborhood by night as well as by day before you choose a new location!

Are you located reasonably near your children's school, your church, and helpful friends or relatives? Are you comfortable with the location, or is it too isolated to suit you? Do the surroundings please you? If you have an apartment, is it among units occupied by neighbors you enjoy? Are fire hazards minimal?

If you plan a change of residence, you have reason to spend adequate time on the problem-solving steps outlined. As guides to your fact-finding process, consumer publications should be studied.

A move to a different part of the country is best preceded by a trial run. Take a vacation there, if you can manage it. Even a dream spot can pose problems. During widowhood I spent winter months of two different years in Arizona, and enjoyed a variety of interesting experiences there. But I resisted the urge to buy property, and have been glad I kept my Midwestern farm home as my headquarters.

Are you hesitant about sharing your residence with one or more relatives, yet desirous of companionship? Few widows seem to find other single women they are able to reside with happily, but it can happen. Two families headed by mothers sometimes team successfully. Space, housekeeping styles, and personalities have to be considered.

A widow's lifetime dependency pattern may lead her into a quick decision to move in with her adult children or to suggest that they move into her home. Studies show that she is unlikely ever to have her own household again. On the other hand, it often happens that a son's or a daughter's family never really establishes itself as a unit when the members move in with "Mom."

When does it work for a widow to live with her children and grandchildren? It works when Grandma is willing for them to live their own lives, when she and those younger are willing to share the cost and work of maintaining the home, and when Grandma leaves the rearing of children to their parents. Having private quarters arranged for members of a three-generation household is essential.

Occasionally a widow who wants people close by finds that owning a duplex and renting half of it to people she enjoys is a good thing. If you want to try this, look for easy upkeep, favorable rent, and tenants you consider trustworthy.

Whatever your residence decision, you will be most contented with the choice if it is possible to keep up the place without having to rely on the help of relatives or friends, if you can entertain others in your favorite ways, and if you can get to the places you like to go with comparative ease.

Repairs, Repairs!

Small repairs often loom as a large worry. Judging from the woes women express, classes on the subject should always be well filled. Learning to care for extension cords, radios, clocks, toilets, drains, and countless small appliances should be on your must list. That is, unless you want to risk becoming unpopular by continually asking for help!

Using the laundromat may be preferable to service calls for

an ailing washer or dryer. When the refrigerator or your heating system needs attention, you have no such easy alternative. Learn all you can about operating appliances correctly. Read the instruction books! Be businesslike when you do call for a repairman. When he comes, ask for an estimate on the cost of parts and labor. If at all possible, obtain service from the store where you purchased the equipment.

Transportation

The small amount you invest in a car-care manual may be very well spent, as you take over responsibility for your own transportation. Public libraries sometimes find it difficult to keep enough such manuals on hand to supply the demand. Some magazines and newspapers publish seasonal tips on the care of your auto, the right tires for your driving style, and how to get safe maximum miles.

One widow's auto dealer taught her how to check her car's oil each night when she and her traveling companions stopped at a motel en route to the Southwest. Whenever she bought gas, she was armed with knowledge of the oil situation. Having also read news reports of rackets by which motorists are tricked into having extensive repairs, she and her passengers took turns going to the rest room. Someone was always with the car, alert for any suspicious acts.

Many of us live where we must chauffeur ourselves if we expect to get about. One of my widow correspondents suggests considering well before you dispose of your car. She sold hers, on the advice of friends concerned about her finances. She found that she was left at the mercy of those few who might now and then offer a ride. A long way from the bus line, she needed her car to shop, to maintain social contacts, and to do volunteer work. For her, the car had spelled the difference between being a well-adjusted woman alone and being dangerously isolated.

When circumstances prevent one's owning and driving a car, serious thought should be given to alternatives. Those who have dependable public transportation are fortunate. Location on a bus line may be your key to independence. Taxis may seem expensive, yet with good planning they can be economical. Scheming to walk a few blocks, ride the bus downtown, do errands, and wind up at the department store or food market where you assemble your load before summoning a taxi, makes it possible to utilize this door-to-door transportation fully.

If you have kind relatives and friends, willing to pick you up for church and meetings, try to stay in their good graces! Your promptness, your consideration of their other responsibilities, and your thoughtfulness in sharing car expense will go a long way. If no money is accepted, a pan of homemade rolls, a dinner out, or some concert tickets might show your appreciation.

Your Health

Your annual or semiannual health examinations and dental checkups are more than ever important if you live alone. Cooling your worries by finding out what causes a symptom, and learning what to do in order to correct or "live with" a condition is vital to peace of mind. Having a doctor you can call for advice, and keeping a good neighbor suitably informed of health problems you have, is reassuring.

Widows who spend much time alone seem to neglect what they should have to maintain good health. Meals may be sadly unbalanced, and little exercise taken. Sleep may be irregular. Setting the table and preparing balanced meals may seem unimportant until you consider the consequences of sketchy eating. Regular outdoor exercise may strike you as "nice but impractical" unless you total up the benefits. Once convinced that diet and exercise goals are important for you, you can set yourself minimal goals, then more challenging ones. Tailor your individual program under your doctor's guidance for best results.

Getting together regularly with several friends to eat well-balanced meals, to enjoy biking, golfing, calisthenics, or brisk walks may be a possibility for you. The fellowship adds zest, and strengthens determination to stay with the schedule.

Prompt attention for emotional illness is recommended. Some widows in need of care from a mental health professional delay going in search of help. Well-meaning friends may remark that the widow is "doing all right" or will be O.K. because she is a "strong person." Both the widow and her friends may know it isn't true. The strains of widowhood are such that help may be required.

Possible sources of help are the Women's Center in your city, the county Mental Health Center, Catholic Social Services, other church social services, and agencies affiliated with Family Service Association of America, 44 East 23d Street, New York, N.Y. 10010 (ask for the address of the agency nearest you).

Security

How can you secure your person, home, and possessions from injury, thievery, or vandalism? Have you checked your security habits to make sure you do not invite trouble? All the safety tips are due for review and new emphasis: lock your house windows and doors, and your car doors; leave a light and a radio turned on when you are away in the evening; care for keys wisely; avoid poorly lighted areas; mark your possessions; remove hazards from your home or property.

Have an adult son or daughter, or a trusted friend, go over safeguards with you, perhaps to discover possible dangers in your environment. At the urging of my older son, I had a security light installed in the farmyard. It not only aided me when I drove in or out but also made it easy to ascertain that the premises were clear of uninvited visitors. I schooled myself to pull shades and close draperies at night. Telephone numbers for the sheriff's office, fire department, doctor, and nearest neighbor were plainly posted.

Any unknown caller at my door was kept outside a locked screen door while I learned the nature of the call. I also kept a few articles of male apparel in view on the porch—a jacket on a hook, a pair of rubber boots, a cap, and gloves. I asked neighbors who might drop in during the evening to telephone first, so that I would be watching for their arrival.

How do you have your name listed in the telephone directory? The listing "Mary L. Smith" plainly indicates a woman alone. "Mrs. John Smith" tells the nuisance caller that the woman is probably a widow. "M. L. Smith" does not reveal the sex of the person listed. At the same time, Mrs. Smith's friends can learn to recognize the initials as those of Mary Louise Smith.

Take all reasonable security measures, then trust that you will probably be safe. You don't need "security overkill." Of course, there is always some danger. Crimes occur in all kinds of locations and all strata of society. Are you willing to be controlled by the possibility of crime? When you have done your best to secure your environment, I hope you can relax. Your life philosophy and your religious faith, as well as your common sense, are tested in the area of personal security.

Sources of Help

There are now many sources of help for meeting problems and making living arrangements. A number have already been mentioned in this chapter. The self-help organizations discussed in Chapter 3 often bring into their meetings speakers with expertise on such subjects as car care, home management, health, and personal safety.

Through university extension programs and workshops in most states, widows learn to be more effective lady landlords, estate planners, homemakers, and/or single parents. At least some of the programs of this kind are probably on your area's extension schedule. Extension tries to anticipate and fill needs. Don't be afraid to ask!

The more habitually you follow logical steps for decision-making, the more confidently you will choose in matters of residence, work, transportation, health, personal security, investment, and giving. You don't have to be helpless about business affairs or living arrangements for long. You can soon learn how to conduct this part of your new life with pride and satisfaction.

9

You and Your Church

How are you feeling toward your church in widowhood? Has the relationship continued much as it was while your husband was living? Or has it changed in ways you did not anticipate? Have you acted to establish your role within the church, or have things simply happened to determine your role?

One widow, whose husband had been a leader of the congregation, felt unable for several years to resume attendance at worship services. Anger toward God and her husband's doctors overcame her whenever she tried to sit in a pew.

Another widow, who had been only a nominal member of her church, began immediately after bereavement to attend worship services, women's meetings, and Bible study. She surprised her friends with her sudden interest and zeal.

A third went to church services and occasional meetings, but felt "different" and uncomfortable in a setting where the focus was primarily on couples and families. She wanted to continue in the fellowship, as in the past, but many signs indicated to her that as a single she no longer fit in.

Counting on Your Church

Surely as a widow you have good reason to count on the church as the resource most likely to extend comfort, emotional support, and spiritual guidance in accordance with your need. Care of the widowed and the orphaned has long been an important mission of the church.

Why, then, do many widows feel alienated from, or at least uncomfortable in, the church? Why do some of them consider the church irrelevant to their lives, especially when many others report they "could never have made it" without their faith and a supportive church fellowship?

Some of the same widows who are quick to express gratitude for the ministrations of church members and pastor during a time of long illness or sudden death of the husband are bewildered by virtual abandonment in the months of aloneness that follow. Did you wonder where all the caring people went? What happened to concern for "those who mourn"?

During a Parents Without Partners discussion I heard a single father say the church "hadn't done him any good," so he quit. Another man remarked that since he would have been attending worship alone, he joined the choir, and found new friends.

Several women and men in the PWP group confessed that they "had to make themselves go to church." Some who found no class designed for adult singles turned to church school teaching. One person tried three different churches because there had been no acceptance of a "single" in his home church, and eventually found a new church home.

Have you been able to put into words what you want from the church, and what you can do as part of the church, during widowhood? Do you see obstacles in the way? What positive factors do you see?

If you are like the majority of widows who have communicated with me, you desire two things: (1) the development of a mutually helpful relationship with your chosen church and (2) the stimulation of your individual spiritual growth. These two can progress hand in hand. It may help to consider what factors are affecting you and the people who are the church.

Most widows remember how little they knew about shock, mourning, and loneliness anxiety before the trauma of mate-loss came to them. Yet they find it hard to excuse others, especially their ministers and church friends, for being unprepared to understand the emotional and practical needs of the bereaved.

As a widow, you probably think that pastors and church members, of all people, ought to know grief's forms, to realize your hurt, to help relieve fears of loneliness, to make allowance for change in economic status, to be aware of the strains of single parenthood. Yet, an anonymous contributor to *THEOS Newsletter* observed: "People see you at church all the time and you're smiling and seem to be doing fine. What they don't realize is the problems you have during the week."[25]

A common complaint is that friendship and encouragement are withdrawn just when the widow most needs them. Church friends, like most others, may be unable to relate to you as a widow supportively. Those tantalizing promises which are not kept—"We will telephone you soon . . . have you over for lunch . . . get together with you for a picnic or for coffee"—can be cruel and inhuman treatment.

Phrasing of announcements in your church's bulletins and newsletters may give the impression that most events scheduled are for those who have spouses and children, rather than for church people as a whole. The phrase "Family Night" may be used, when "Fellowship Night" would be more accurate and inclusive.

Insensitivity to the feelings of the widowed and other singles is demonstrated by the exclusive naming of adult classes and groups, for example, Mr. and Mrs. Club or Couples Class. The emphasis in sermons, discussions, and meetings of church organizations in many communities is chiefly upon the married couple and what is considered the "complete" family. Your hackles may rise if you constantly hear reference to the single-parent family as "a broken home," when you and your children feel you are achieving wholeness despite your loss.

Your talents and labors, like those of other singles, may be readily accepted by the church fellowship, always hungry for doers. But your personhood may be ignored or even rejected by the same folks who like to have your help with their pet church projects.

There is some foundation for charges that the clergy fail to minister adequately to widows. Pastors, rabbis, and priests often lack basic understanding of widowhood. They sometimes fail to give the widowed sufficient time to develop needed dialogue. You may agree with widows who have observed that they were offered a few platitudes rather than empathy. The clergy, like the laity, may back off when getting involved is uncomfortable.

But in defense of the clergy, it should be noted that more is often expected of them than it is humanly possible to deliver. They do have their own physical, emotional, social, and professional limitations. Even when they have strength, time, and concern for their widowed parishioners, they may be hampered by obstacles unrecognized by "the flock."

If you were past the age of sixty when you became a widow, you may be speedily received into a grouping of church friends who are experienced in widowhood. You are welcome, and you accept your role within the church fellowship with little change, perhaps, from what you knew in the past.

But in small congregations, a younger widow may find no one in her age bracket who is widowed and able to empathize. A few elderly widows who "talk gloom" to you can be depressing. Thank God if you are in touch with widows who have faith and optimism!

Try to put aside your unrealistic expectations of those in the church who have had no experience similar to yours. But if people of your church unwittingly tend to "put widows in their place," you may be able to help change their attitudes. Widowed persons need to be part of the common life of the church fellowship rather than "special cases."

You can be glad that we are currently seeing development of some positive factors that can lead to a mutually helpful relationship between the widow and her church:

1. True koinonia, in which all members' needs are shared and met as fully as possible, and in which every person counts, regardless of marital status.
2. Increasing awareness of widowhood feelings and problems on the part of people in the church, through reading, dialogue, and discussion.
3. New willingness of the widow to widen her friendship circle.
4. Specific planning to meet widowhood needs.

As a widow you stand to benefit from emphasis on genuine koinonia, as do the unmarried, the divorced, and also the married. In a time when there are many singles, the church is belatedly recognizing social trends, and awakening to the needs of people who are not "coupled." Better yet, in many instances the church fellowship is accepting and including persons as sisters and brothers, each having unique worth.

As loving acceptance increases, more effort is made to understand feelings. When there is grief, it is worked through in an atmosphere of caring. You are fortunate if you belong to a church that keeps in touch with your needs.

While you are feeling grateful for such care, remember your own part in the relationship. Are you as concerned for others as they are for you? Are you open to new friendships in the church? Are you perhaps helping to initiate or support an organization for the widowed?

Your Spiritual Growth in Widowhood

Your first reaction to the suggestion that you can grow spiritually during widowhood may be an angry retort that the cost of such development has already been too great! What woman wants to be widowed in order to benefit her soul?

Yet the crisis of mate-loss signals a period when you, the survivor, need as never before to draw upon the Creator's marvelous powers of strengthening and refining a human being. Whether or not the desire to raise spiritual sights exists at the outset, it may arise as the feelings and experiences of widowhood affect you in unexpected ways.

If you feel you have not made much progress in this area, it may be important for you to recognize some obstacles to spiritual growth in widowhood, which often block positive change:

1. Serious delay in accomplishing grief work.
2. Failure to obtain professional care when it is needed to regain physical and/or emotional health.
3. Inadequate, distorting, or limiting theological concepts.
4. Lack of openness to new spiritual ideas and learning.
5. Unwillingness to try a group or activity new to you.
6. Failure to set priorities for worship, study, and reading to stimulate spiritual growth.

The first two obstacles in the list were discussed in Chapter 2. The inadequate, distorting, or limiting theological concepts listed next may have stayed with you from early religious training, or its lack, in home or church. For instance, you may have held the idea that prayer for recovery from illness or injury is unanswered unless the patient regains health. Or you may have a distorted concept of the dimensions of faith. Are you troubled by the idea that your faith was insufficient, and that as a consequence you lost your husband? Do you suffer from the notion that you did not have "faith enough" to pray your mate through his illness successfully?

Regarding the other three obstacles listed, are you remembering that an environment in which spiritual growth can take place is vital? You are in a better position than anyone else to create that environment. It is possible to avoid or ignore all religious opportunities. But you can decide to expose your mind to the inspirations God sends humans in various ways. You can choose to commune regularly with the Source of all understanding and all strength.

What are some of the positive factors for your spiritual growth in widowhood? My list includes:

1. *The "cry for help"*

Whatever the circumstances of your mate-loss, and whatever your spiritual status at the time, you must have raised that cry for help so characteristic of a widow's bereavement responses. C. S. Lewis wrote: "The time when there is nothing at all in your soul except a cry for help may be just the time when God can't give it: you are like the drowning man who can't be helped because he clutches and grabs."[26] When we have the capacity to receive help, God gives help to us. That capacity, which may be temporarily lacking, may enable us a little later on to begin to accept the help God faithfully provides.

The first positive factor for spiritual growth in widowhood is to admit that help is needed and desired. When we are trying to be strong, in and of ourselves, we are not really ready to grow. You might say we have to be "brought low" for the seed of our growth to be planted. After that we have to become receptive to the light, the warmth, the living water, and the nutrients that can stimulate our growth.

2. *Realization of spiritual needs*

In widowhood we have the need to know God better. As we mourn, as we seek perspective for our grief, and as we become receptive toward God's ways of answering our earnest prayers, we desire to know God more fully. Is your communion with God becoming richer? Have you sensed a closeness greater than you knew before?

My own bereavement experience made me more keenly aware of God's nearness. In those first moments of shock and uncertainty following our accident, I knew my husband was seriously injured, but did not realize that his death had been instantaneous. I held an umbrella over us both with one hand, and found a pressure point on Carl's temple with the other, trying to control the bleeding. While waiting for the ambulance I prayed aloud constantly, asking God over and over to help Carl.

I had a strong sense of there being three persons rather than two beside the wrecked car in the rain. I felt sure of God's presence with us.

When the actions and facial expressions of those who came to our aid silently told me Carl had died, I continued to feel that God was there, sharing my sorrow. My "Help Carl" prayers were being answered in a way quite different from what I had expected. Though dazed and numb, I somehow felt assured that God was indeed helping my husband achieve transition into a new life.

In the days that followed I felt also a strong identification with God's Son, who suffered as we humans suffer, who knew the preciousness of human ties, who experienced human agonies of separation.

Several years later, climaxing intensive study of the book of Psalms in a continuing education class, I felt moved to compose my own psalm of retrospect:

> To Thee, O Lord, be thanksgiving and praise!
> To Thee my full gratitude is due—
> Who hast been present with me
> In all my experiences—
> Who hast shown mercy, and
> Bestowed new blessings upon me,
> Even beside the highway of death,
> Even in the valley of loneliness,
> In the dark privacy of grief,
> And in the heart of the congregation.

3. *Laying guilt before God*

Whether or not we admit it to any of our human companions, most of us feel some kind of guilt in bereavement. Have you been able to examine yours and lay it before God? Feelings of having done too little to express love for your spouse, or of having somehow failed to provide the exact medical and nursing care required for recovery, may be easier to admit before God than anger toward him who "let" your husband die.

Anger toward God often stems from a concept of God as an authoritarian deity who decides at a certain time to snatch a person away from earthly life. It does not arise from knowing God as a merciful father who unfailingly guides the person's transition into the next experience when this life terminates. But it may arise from saying piously, "This death was God's will," while believing God would be cruel indeed to will the death.

Since your loss, you may have been saying in essence: "There must be a reason for this. God must have a purpose, but I can't see it." Translated, this says: "I couldn't stand losing my husband, except that my loss is evidently necessary in order to fulfill God's master plan. I cannot grasp the plan, because it transcends human understanding. The unthinkable thought would be that my husband died for no reason."

To console yourself, you may also have been saying, "My husband died because it was 'his time to go.' His unseen calendar of life was marked. God's alarm clock was set." Yet your logic insists: "My husband died because his human body could not survive his injuries or his illness any longer. God's natural laws set the boundaries of what the body can stand. Those boundaries were exceeded. Therefore my husband died."

As you put into words your guilt feelings, your attempted explanations, and finally your reasoned account of the death, you may be enabled to receive either the forgiveness or the greater understanding God invariably offers us when we confess guilt.

4. *Search for identity as a single person*

One thoughtful widow wrote to me, "God will help you, but he expects much." She seemed to be in the process of discovering how she could be an effective witness to her Christian faith in widowhood. You can also grow spiritually as you seek purpose for your life following bereavement. There are others on earth who need you. How wonderful that God will lead you to discover them!

If you have known the assurance of God's direction in your life previously, you will be all the more ready to seek it in the period ahead. If your life has not been dedicated to God in the past, it can be from now on.

A widower's prayer well expresses the sorrow, the guilt, the needs, and the desire to find new purpose in living singly, as he felt them:

THE LOSS OF A MATE

She was so precious to me, O Lord,
and now you have taken her from me.
Oh how I loved her, Lord, and needed her!
Next to you, I loved her more than
anyone or anything I have ever known.
There were times when
she was more important to me than you and your
purposes for my life.
And there were far more occasions
when I placed my selfish concerns
far ahead of my love and concern for her.
I pray that you will cover my guilt,
O Lord.
She was your gift to me, my God,
without the guarantee that I would
have her forever.
I am grateful, Lord—
even while my heart cries out in
bitterness.
Forgive me that I cannot joyfully
Commit her into your hands.
Nevertheless I do so—reluctantly—
and I pray that your miracle-working grace

will put me together again,
that you will fill the empty places
in my life,
and renew, encourage, and
strengthen me.
She has left me, Lord, but you
haven't.
Put my feet in motion again,
O Lord,
that I may continue to walk in
your paths
and carry on your purposes.[27]

5. *Mature use of prayer*

The quality of your prayer life reveals the degree of awareness you have concerning your own special needs in widowhood. It is also a good indicator of the extent of your progress through grief toward a steady state. Have you prayed more, or less, since you became a widow? Have you prayed frantically for help? Have you cried out to God frequently, but failed to listen and watch for answers?

Perhaps you have surprised yourself by leaving off complaints, and thanking God for years of fulfilling marriage, for children, for employment, for daily strength, for all the blessings you can count. Perhaps you have progressed past informing God of where and how he is needed to being grateful for his dependable presence in every aspect of life.

Is your greatest need now for guidance and strength in decision-making? Are you burdened and somewhat frightened by the weight of unfamiliar responsibilities? Are you trying to choose wisely, yet floundering? One plan for problem-solving is suggested in Chapter 8. Praying for God's help as you take the steps outlined is mature use of prayer.

To sum up, your relationship with your church can be helpful both to you and to the church fellowship. Both you and the church's other people may need to do some changing in order to communicate and to see possibilities.

You may be turned off by the very suggestion of spiritual growth in widowhood until the cries for help and the unburdening of your guilt, real or imagined, free you to desire a new closeness to God. You will surely shed some immature and inadequate religious concepts as you reach out and grow in spirit. Prayer will have new, unexpected validity in your widowhood experience. Despite your doubts and disillusionments, you can eventually rejoice to discover that you *are* developing spiritually!

10

Dating and Socializing

Middle-agers brave enough to begin dating are often subjects for gossipy attention. This makes them give up or seek to conceal a budding friendship. Widowers and bachelors may withhold friendship they would like to offer, for fear a woman they would befriend or persons in the community might take it too seriously.

Fear that your actions may be misinterpreted may inhibit you from extending a simple invitation, doing a neighborly act, or drawing several lonely persons together for informal visiting. You may be unduly sensitive to what others will say—or to what you think they will say! It would help if neighbors in the community would simply assume that adult friendships *are* friendships, *not* necessarily leading to marriage.

Because we met on a church-sponsored tour of England, and later saw each other at semiannual Archives-History Commission meetings away from our home communities, John (my second husband) and I were able to observe each other over a two-year period without social pressures. Our actual dating began after this period of gradual acquaintance.

Are you still wearing your wedding ring? Some men do not ask to date a widow who gives this sign that she still thinks of herself as "married." You may wear the ring, as many do, to remind yourself of precious memories. Or you may consider it "protection" in some circumstances. But it could turn off the interest of a man you would enjoy knowing better.

Men who have lost their wives through death are often wary. If there is a flicker of interest in future companionship, the man will likely wait for an opportunity to test it, in some safe, prosaic setting. Thoughtful, responsible males may prefer to observe widows at a respectful distance until they are reasonably sure they want friendship to develop.

Andrew L., a widower, described his uncomfortable feelings when receiving mail from desperately lonely widows who were bidding for attention. One woman used the device of pretending to write in behalf of a widow friend.

A wiser widow wrote to me: "I have observed in some friends' lives that a desperate man hunt is *not* the answer to loneliness. I would say a *self* hunt accomplishes more. . . . Once you have found *yourself* and made a satisfactory life, you might even find someone you could share it with. But my observation is that it should be in that order."

Evelyn Mumaw, author of *Woman Alone*, asserts that "a happily married woman may be very mature in her Christian experience, but if her husband dies and their relationship has been a satisfying one, she is going to have some unmet drives and hungers."[28] Not many widows have the same readiness to confide their sexual feelings that they have to expose their problems of business, child-rearing, or aloneness. If you truly enjoyed the sexual partnership, and knew the deep comfort of intimacy in your marriage, it is a serious hardship to adjust to life without it.

If, instead, you happen to be a widow who looked upon sex life as duty rather than pleasure and fulfillment, you may feel relieved that there are no longer any such demands upon you.

Many of us have grown up assuming that in widowhood sexual desires and energies are to be stifled, if not ignored. In early bereavement, fatigue may have kept you less aware of sexual tension than usual. Then, when body and mind began to strengthen, a surge of loyalty toward the mate who died may have swept away the thought of being sexually deprived.

But ours is a sexually stimulating society. As a widow, you may be thinking hitherto unthinkable thoughts. You may be astonished at some of your fantasies. At times you may be angry at God for providing you with sexual vigor but no acceptable outlet.

Making your way through today's maze of sexual choices may prove more of a challenge than you had supposed. When you feel lacking in emotional support, it may help to talk with other widows who have learned how to handle their feelings comfortably. Taking time to find those who are good sounding boards—able to help you accept yourself and deal with yourself—is time well spent. However your sexuality is expressed, let the choice be your own.

Cultivating a wide circle of friends of various ages and interests is a helpful way to cope with your sex drive. Current literature and drama notwithstanding, intimate relationships are not necessarily sexual! We all need closeness to others. Why be scared off from close friendships by the now-popular notion that some kind of sexual action is invariably involved? You can remember that, as one single put it, "there is nothing really wrong with you if you lack 'sex life' for a period or always."

Sexual activity, engaged in prematurely, can actually shut off other ways of communicating. A potentially meaningful relationship may be stunted as a result. Quickly resorting to sexual intercourse can be a cop-out for those who are really in need of interaction through intellectual and recreational sharing.

If you don't want to be a user or an abuser sexually speaking, you have every reason to be a refuser. If "dinner and bed" dating is not your style, you can show yourself to be discriminating, holding out for a solidly based friendship with someone who shares your ideals.

It isn't easy to say "No, thank you" to a dating offer. You may be quite confident that you would never be stampeded into an ill-advised marriage or extramarital sex. But you could be in bondage to a weekly dinner engagement with a man you know you can't become serious about. You could be tied to a card game that bores you on a regular basis, by simply failing to consider whether you are saying "Yes" to one evening or to a whole series.

Many singles of both sexes are successfully sublimating their sexual drives in other kinds of creative acts, for example, in music, art, writing, community action, or friendship to people with special needs. I discovered that prayer for ability to deal with feelings can help. A good balance between physical work and recreation and pouring creative energies into my writing also helped me immeasurably.

Evelyn Mumaw, who experienced both the frustrations of single womanhood and the satisfactions of a happy marriage, recommended several positive actions to the Christian "woman alone": Discipline yourself to avoid situations and activities that you find sexually stimulating. . . . Change activities when you discover that you are being stimulated to the point of frustration. . . . Commit the sexual part of your being to the keeping power of God in the dedication of your total self to Him.[29]

How Can You "Socialize" Now?

Life as a single will mean developing your own ways of associating with others. One area of decision will probably involve membership in clubs, civic groups, and church organizations. Did you belong to too many groups as a couple? Too few? Did you belong only to groups your husband wanted to join? Did you forego membership in a drama club or a music club because it interested only you, not your mate?

Judging for yourself is the key to choosing membership in any group. When you are alone and able to assess your social needs and desires, it is a good technique to plot out daily, weekly, and seasonal schedules, also to list groups that truly appeal to you. Consider the direction you want your personal growth and your community service to take. Transportation and membership costs may make a difference. You (not your family or friends) need to do the choosing.

There is a hazard for the widowed person in overjoining. Too many membership commitments may result in a hectic schedule, a fatigued body, and a cluttered mind. Deliberate overjoining to keep busy probably indicates an unhealthy escapism from the fears of the single life.

Many books written for those who live singly are filled with tips and suggestions for entertaining. You may lack confidence for inviting mixed groups and fall into a pattern of inviting only women. It takes more ingenuity to devise good ways of bringing married friends together when you live alone. You may discover that inviting one married couple at a time leaves the man without much part in the conversation. However, when two couples are invited to dinner, the men and their wives are all more comfortable and free to enjoy fellowship.

Rebecca J. is a widow who has successfully maintained friendships with many of the married couples she and her husband chummed with. She says that these friends are very thoughtful about including her in their good times. But she made it clear at the outset that she would go to dinner or a show with them only if it were understood that she would pay her own way. They accepted her terms willingly.

Learning to go out socially without a male escort or a woman companion is part of your personal growth as a widow. Being dependent on others controls your friendships, and prevents you from the experimentation that could help you grow.

When you go out to eat alone, you can learn to enter a restaurant with an air of self-assurance and the expectation of being a valued customer rather than just a "woman alone." A few snobbish restaurants may refuse to seat a woman alone or may give unescorted women poor service. But your own friendly manner, your expectation of being well treated, and your tipping as generously as you can when you are pleased will go far toward generating courtesy and consideration.

Noontime may prove a friendlier, more informal time to have a meal out than the evening dinner hour. In both small-town and urban settings one can frequently find unpaired people and casual groupings of working folks in the cafés at midday. After church on Sundays, couples or families often hailed me over to sit at their tables when I walked into the restaurant alone. I soon lost my earlier shyness and ate out often, glad when others asked me to join them, but able to enjoy a meal alone when there was no opportunity for fellowship.

Handling the holidays is a special problem for the widowed or single parents. On special days, which your family always celebrated in a warm and happy way, feelings of isolation may powerfully recur. The usual quick recipe for turning such thoughts around is learning to initiate new or modified ways of filling these times.

If you have growing children, there is good reason to maintain a number of family traditions begun when your husband was alive. You may also seek with the children some new ways to express holiday meanings. For example, helping to host international visitors or students from other countries can broaden horizons and bring satisfaction.

If weekdays, with their well-filled schedules, seem better to you than "blank Saturdays or Sundays," you may want to consider some new, positive planning to help you anticipate the weekends. Determine the reasons you dread Saturdays and Sundays. Make changes that will give these days a new look!

Two or more single-parent families sometimes discover that banding together for holiday observances or weekend fun can restore much of the glow they thought had been dimmed forever. Whether such plans are organization-sponsored or spontaneous among friends, the idea often catches on.

If your children are now grown and living in distant places, you need not feel that getting together with them for each holiday is the only desirable way to celebrate. Cheering the lives of persons living nearby can lead to very fulfilling experiences.

Controlling Your Own Social Life

Many protests are heard about those who avoid widows, but few about those who rush in to fill the vacuum created by spouse-loss. You may have to be firm toward your own well-meaning parents, your husband's parents, your brothers, sisters, or adult children who would "infantilize" you. Being treated as a child—an infant in widowhood, you might say—can keep you from your developmental tasks.

If you have a family of fatherless children, loving grandparents may logically figure in plans for supplying some of the needed care or recreational companionship. But you can seek a good balance of self-reliance on the part of your single-parent family, with some supportiveness on the part of relatives.

If your children are "out of the nest," you may be highly susceptible to your parents' urgings that you reside with them. This might result in putting all of their needs ahead of your own. Though still youthful in tastes and interests, you may be influenced to participate in your parents' social groups. You may miss opportunities to cultivate friendship with people of your own age. Your time may be too filled with your parents' schedule for you to live a life of your own.

Harriet T., a middle-aged widow, maintained her separate residence half a mile away from the mother's centrally located apartment. The daughter wisely limited her visits and chauffering to a few mutually agreed upon times each week. By giving each other plenty of time apart, these two were able to enjoy fully the time they spent together. Each had freedom to move about in and widen her own circle of friends.

Submitting to the domination of a relative in financial matters or housing can lead to further loss of your independence through control of your social contacts. Such patterns are often established in the weeks when one is too fatigued and too confused to protest. It may prove traumatic for all concerned when you realize that you *do* want to control your own social life after all.

Some widows take courses in assertiveness training, to be able to act independently. Others recover enough of their dormant self-reliance to resume command without outside help. Some bereaved families may need the help of counselors to support them in making choices and decisions, in achieving a balance of closeness with relatives *and* self-reliance. In any case, having control over your human relationships is vital to growth.

11

Should You Remarry?

You may already have answered "yes" or "no" to the question of remarriage. Your answer may have been a statement confided to a friend, or perhaps an unspoken thought. You may have blurted out to someone a hopeless, "I know *I'll* never remarry." Or perhaps you have maintained a discreet silence on the subject, while secretly wishing an attractive new man might appear out of the blue and rescue you from widowhood.

You may not have answered an outright "yes" or "no," but a less certain "possibly," "maybe," or "that would depend. . . ." You may not want to rule out a second marriage entirely, even though you have learned to recognize values in singlehood and to accept it as your new status. How can one "think sense" about the question of remarriage?

Is it normal to continue feeling intense loyalty to your deceased husband? Should you face the possibility that you will never have a good opportunity to remarry? Do you pretend that you aren't one bit interested, when you are? If you *do* have chances to date, should you be prepared with your own screening standards for accepting or refusing?

All these questions and many others may be valid for you to raise as you progress toward the womanhood of your future years. Working through to your view of remarriage will involve some examination of the feelings you and your first mate had in this area. Did you and he ever discuss second marriage? Was there support for a second marriage in case one of you was left alone?

Were there expressions of jealousy, of trying to control, even from the grave? Could you honestly encourage each other to feel that an interest in second marriage would be natural for those who knew deep satisfaction in the first marriage experience? Was some rash promise given that there "could never be anyone else"? Was it given at a time when neither of you had any way of understanding how you would feel after bereavement? Are friends right when they say it is a compliment to the first spouse if a person remarries?

If the married state has previously been satisfying for you, and you hope for a second marriage, you may feel discouraged. The ratio of eligible men to eligible women is sharply lower by the time one reaches the middle years. If you are younger, and have children to rear, your concern for the effect of a second marriage upon them may eliminate a number of possible choices.

Do you believe that continuing single is better than risking a disappointing marriage? Have you made a go of it as a single person, proving to yourself and others that you are able to conduct your own life? Have you shown that you can appreciate and make the most of life, whether married or not?

A widow who is a career executive declares, "Most widows I know don't want to remarry." Somewhat scornfully, another widow, who has dated often, says, "All the men ask me, 'Do you like to cook?' " Having grown accustomed to an independence they never had before, many widows surveyed in professional study indicated that they had no interest in marrying again. Others, after tragic loss of the first husband, feared to risk loving—and perhaps losing—again.

Statistics show a much smaller number of men in proportion to women who are hoping to remarry. But some positive conclusions can be drawn from studies of widowed persons. The widowed who do marry again have an excellent chance for achieving happy marriage.

Taking into account the pronounced shortage of men they would actually consider marrying, however, I think widows stand to enjoy greater peace of mind when they assume remarriage to be unlikely. Rebuilding their lives as singles, and valuing friendship with men, apart from marriage potential, are within the possibilities for all widows.

Meeting Eligible Men

One of the commonest complaints heard from women who admit their interest in a second marriage is that it is difficult to meet eligible men and to "become available." Some of those who complain most do the least about their predicament. If you enjoy a good mix of your longtime favorite activities with several new interests, you place yourself in company with other people of similar tastes. You are then more apt to meet congenial companions.

Trying to "make it happen" through aggressiveness, lonely hearts clubs, computer dating, and the like has proved disappointing for many. Those who make a business of searching, or who pay others to search for them, seldom are rewarded according to their wishes. It is true that there are some introduction services in which reputable, understanding people earnestly endeavor to match persons of similar age, interest, and background. But commercial enterprise to provide dating partners and possible marriage partners seems to produce more woe than pleasing results.

To appear to be interested in eligible men, but not actively searching, is not easy. The person who advised, "Look, but never look like you're looking" may have meant, "Keep your eyes open, check out possibilities, but don't be obvious." Being involved in an activity you enjoy, and chancing to find someone you would like to know better—without taking direct responsibility to "make it happen"—is a more likely way to meet a new friend than deliberate hunting.

How can you increase your availability? Probably by: (1)

selectively volunteering your know-how or help in church or civic projects that interest you, (2) joining interest groups and organizations that have meaning for you, (3) being a welcome guest, (4) inviting others to your home or for "evenings out," remembering to keep the atmosphere cheerful, (5) traveling, if you enjoy it, and (6) attending such functions as class reunions and other gatherings of men and women near your age.

As part of your "new growth," you can recapture lost dating skills. Showing your interest in others' ideas and suggestions may eventually produce invitations to share experience. Becoming more aware of fascinating places to go and things to do will prepare you to make suggestions when you have opportunities.

You may decide to indicate your willingness to share costs of recreation some of the time. You may even initiate some dates by having tickets in hand. Men who have been married a long time, and then widowed, often say they are hesitant to ask for a date. They fear they have "forgotten how to court a woman." Being friendly in a way that is reassuring and kind, but not forward, is a dating skill with which you can be supportive of the man who shows signs of interest in you.

Making the most of your own personable qualities, showing enthusiasm for hobbying or recreation, dressing and grooming yourself attractively, and having a ready smile are indicators that you are apt to be pleasant company. No doubt you are happiest with people who set you at ease, who share your interests, who make you feel desirable and admired. It is the same for the man you would like to have as a dating partner. He isn't likely to pay you any attention if you make him feel uncomfortable or unnoticed.

Do you need any cautions about dating strangers? All those romantic stories of finding a new mate by sheer accident notwithstanding, you should know that widows *are* often the victims of confidence men. Dates with someone whose background you do not know are risky. If you feel doubt about a man who asks you to go with him, you need fuller acquaintance with his motivations. This warning may strike you as quite unnecessary for a supposedly mature woman who is now a widow. But news accounts of widows' being gently swindled are too common to be laughed away.

That Screening Process

Screening and choosing a new person who might become your mate is important at any age. Whether or not you followed such a procedure consciously when you married the first time, you can do it quite deliberately now.

You may be determined that any man who wins you now must measure up to your memory of the first spouse. But it will be impossible to find a man just like your beloved first husband, minus his few faults. Any new man will be different. He will be himself.

If you expect perfection, you don't really intend to remarry at all. You want to live with your selective memories of your first husband. If you expect to find a suitable man who has no annoying habits, no personal flaws, and no loyalty to his deceased wife, you must know you are too demanding. You are making sure that you don't marry again.

If you are more realistic, how can you be sufficiently discriminating? How can you be prepared to accept a date with a man you think you may like, and also to refuse politely the attentions of others you probably wouldn't care for? Have you thought about developing your own screening process?

Shirley M., a widow who sensed a man's interest and realized that he might soon be suggesting a date, jotted down what had impressed her as she observed him: lively interest in people and events, physical and mental vigor, thoughtfulness, attractive appearance, generosity. She felt ready to say "yes" if he asked her to go to dinner or a play. After seeing him in several settings —at committee meetings, on sponsored tours, and in conversational groups—she was convinced that they had much in common.

What are some standards you might use in such screening? They could include: (1) mutual interests; (2) compatible religious and cultural backgrounds; (3) openness, willingness to grow; (4) ability to communicate, to share decisions; (5) attractiveness to you as an individual—perhaps based on vitality, appearance, personality, and sex appeal; and (6) financial stability, as contrasted with irresponsible fiscal attitudes. Add, subtract, or develop your own special standards from scratch—preferably before any dating begins!

The question When should a widow marry? is probably best answered by saying she should marry when anyone else should marry: when she has found a person with whom living will be fuller and happier—a person who is also eligible and willing to share her life.

More often, the real, unasked question is: When is it too soon for a widow to remarry? A widow is not ready to marry again when escape from aloneness is sought, when grief has not been worked through, or when love of the deceased spouse still dominates her thinking. Until she has progressed through widowhood and achieved a relatively steady state in her new womanhood, she is incapable of loving a new and different person enough to marry.

It may be apparent to others that a widow is not ready if she hastily chooses someone quite unsuitable, or if she agrees to marry but keeps finding reasons to delay the plans. It is too soon to marry when emotions are wavering and calm thinking is not possible.

Likewise, it is too soon to marry when the prospective husband is seeking escape, is unable to work through his grief, or is thinking of the prospective wife as a substitute for the wife he lost rather than as a new person to love. We may laugh at the marriage proposal offered by one widower: "Would you like to take Dorothy's place?" But there is serious cause for postponing a second marriage when the first has not yet ended.

In *For You Departed,* Alan Paton revealed his hurt when Dorrie told him, "There is one thing you must understand clearly, and that is that I shall never love you as I loved my husband." The twenty-eight-year-old widow who became Paton's wife continued to wear her first wedding ring after their marriage, not realizing how this made her second husband feel.

Paton observed years later, after Dorrie's death, that she spoke and acted "out of ignorance of the nature of love" when she wore the first marriage ring after her second marriage. A widower himself at age sixty-four, he wrote: "In true love one gives oneself, and it does not matter if one has given oneself before. If I were to marry again, and for love, I would say to the woman, 'I have given myself before, and now I give myself again, with no withholding, and will love and cherish you.' "[30]

When are you too old to marry? Is marriage only for the young and for propagation? Are your relatives and friends right when they argue against marriage for you, or belittle the idea that you could be happily married the second time?

You may be one who has much to bring to marriage. Before labeling yourself "too old," consider what you have to give.

W. C. McKain, in his University of Connecticut study of one hundred older couples, found that three fourths of the older marriages were highly successful, while the remaining one fourth were moderately successful. In general these elderly couples had better health, higher and more secure incomes, and greater mobility than ever before. They had much to bring to the marriage partnership.

In a large number of cases, the couples in the study were already related by marriage. Most of the one hundred couples had known each other before widowhood. Some had been childhood sweethearts. They tended to have similar backgrounds, to be close in age, and to have had successful first marriages. Their added insights aided their later marriages.[31]

Some persons actually are "too old to marry." They are unwilling to make adjustments to another's ways and preferences. Chronological age is not the true indicator, but mental and emotional age. A forty-five-year-old may be too old to yield on any points, while a man or a woman of seventy may be quite young at heart, flexible, and fully capable of appreciating life with a second mate.

Your Children's Feelings About Your Possible Remarriage

Your children's feelings about your possible new marriage may be a strong influence upon your decision. Although you have worked through your grief, your children may continue to have an almost fierce loyalty to their deceased father. You may have to struggle with guilt feelings when leaving your children with a sitter to pursue your own needs through dating.

The children may become rivals of your dating partner or intended spouse. Widows and potential mates often give up trying to bring about a good relationship with a potential stepchild. To help children handle their negative feelings, honest reassurance of their unique places in the family and in your affection is vital. Genuine and patient concern by you and your partner may bring eventual adjustment. Unhurried building of friendship between the children and the possible new father may prepare both for a permanent relationship. In some instances, children express approval of the mother's dating, but balk at the idea of her marriage and the changes involved for them. Adults should realize the extent to which children feel threatened when someone new lays claim to the affections of their surviving parent. After the trauma of bereavement, it is often hard for them to invest in a new child-parent relationship.

One former widow wrote of the difficult testing she went through when she married a man with a teen-age son still at home. Her own children were married and living in distant places. The stepson did not accept her. She was disturbed by his inconsiderate manners, by his extravagance in buying records, sports equipment, and expensive clothes, and by his rowdy friends who came to the house. The marriage was unstable until the son eventually established himself in his own home and career.

Once in a while there may be a fairly simple solution to a youngster's unnerving criticism of the new mother's ways. The book *Living in Step* tells of one stepmother's struggle to woo her young stepson by matching his memory of his first Mom's chili. She tried one version after another, "but he always managed to convey that whatever the recipe, the result just wasn't as good as Mom's.

"The child's craving for 'good' chili continued; the stepmother's enthusiasm for cooking chili did not. One day, she gave up and bought chili in the can. The result?

" 'Hey! This is just like Mom's! You finally made it!' "[32]

Sexual Feelings in Second Marriage

Consideration of your sexual feelings is important as you look at the possibility of a second marriage. Perhaps your sexual desire has built up during widowhood until your expectations in this area are very strong. Are you able to recognize and to discuss these feelings with the prospective mate in such a way that there is mutual understanding? What are his feelings and attitudes? Are his hopes and desires harmonious with yours?

You may have suppressed sexual interest during widowhood, while feeling latent sexual tension. To you it may be surprising to find that you can feel excitement as great as when you were younger. A seven-year widow in her late fifties, calling to announce wedding plans to some close friends, sounded like a sixteen-year-old girl though she was a dignified career woman. She later commented that satisfying sex life can be one of the delightful benefits of second marriage.

How can it be that many people do find as great or greater sexual harmony in the second marriage than they knew in the first? For one thing, a happy first marriage augurs well for the second. Experience is significant. Second mates are often observed to be more thoughtful, considerate, and expressive than they were earlier in their lives.

This mellowing and deeper understanding, coupled with a more selfless, less demanding attitude toward the mate lays a foundation for truer sharing sexually.

When pregnancy is no longer a concern, the wife especially may be enabled to give herself more freely. She may also be loving and understanding when affection is expressed in other ways than intercourse.

Greater privacy when children are grown and gone, more time for sharing a variety of interests, and a more leisurely living pace in many second marriages combine to provide a rich basis for sexual harmony. Gentleness and patience, which flower in middle and later years, are marvelously effective qualities for lovers.

Merely meeting the legal requirements for blood tests is not enough for a premarital physical examination. At the very least, the marrying couple need to have complete physicals and to discuss with each other the details of their current health status. A couple who understand each other's strengths and weaknesses can help each other avoid stresses and strains. Being supportive of each other's needs for suitable diet, exercise, and rest often prevents serious illness from developing. Until improved medical counseling for later marriages is available, it will be necessary for thoughtful couples to make up some of the deficiency by their own study of reliable information and their persistence in seeing that their doctors make thorough premarital examinations.

Other Concerns in Remarriage

It may help to mention a number of the other possible concerns in any consideration of remarriage. Negative feelings should be faced and carefully examined. Is there doubt that one of the partners has progressed in widowhood and singlehood to a point of readiness for the return to paired living? Are you feeling suspicious that your prospective mate is really seeking a cook, a housekeeper, a nurse, rather than a partner in social, recreational, and spiritual activity?

Are you satisfied that the basic feelings you have about marriage are sufficiently compatible with the basic feelings your potential mate has? Have you radically different value systems? Are there serious barriers that should be faced?

Will your money habits need reordering if you are to live in harmony? Have you discussed with your attorney the possibility of an antenuptial agreement to insure that your estate will be inherited by your children and his estate by his children, if these are your desires? After you marry, it is too late to sign an *ante*nuptial agreement!

Whatever your finances and those of your prospective husband, it is simply good sense to tailor your plans for sharing your resources *before* you take any vows. Working out some of the details of joint expense when there are separate incomes is good preparation for harmonious living. When individual checking and savings accounts are maintained, as well as a joint household account, both husband and wife can enjoy the freedom of purchasing clothing, hobby equipment, or gifts from independent funds.

So much attention is focused upon what one stands to receive in a second marriage that the question What can I contribute to this marriage? may be overlooked. Unless you consider your possible contributions to the union, and feel that you do have much to bring to the marriage, you better reconsider the whole matter.

Will you be contributing love, affection, and supportiveness to your husband? He has a right to all of these, ahead of any other considerations. Will you bring companionship with your caring? Will you bring not only your own interests but a genuine interest in your spouse's interests?

If there will be children in the home, can you contribute parenting strengths and know-how? Are you a reasonably skilled homemaker? Will you add strength in the performance of tasks such as transportation, for example, trading off as driver on trips you make together? Are you willing to share whatever economic advantage you may have?

Will you be able to share spiritually and intellectually with your new spouse? Do you care about enough of the same life concerns to be able to share conversationally?

What you expect to receive by entering into your second marriage will probably be similar to gifts you may also bestow: affirming love, supportiveness, affection, companionship, caring. If you have children to rear, you are no doubt hoping your new husband will help in the many aspects of parenting. As a practical homemaker, you may be anticipating help with heavier tasks you have had to struggle with, hire done, or let go during widowhood. Perhaps you are counting on that new spouse's business and management skills to bolster yours, belatedly acquired. Maybe you are going to be relieved to have your husband take charge of auto maintenance, lawn and garden, and small appliance repair.

But remember that few men shine in all these departments. You are not choosing a handyman-baby-sitter-chauffeur-accountant to "live in," but a man whose life you will share in a new, meaningful way. Marrying to "get" is as deplorable the second time as the first. Marrying because one is insecure, helpless, afraid of loneliness, or unable to cope singly is unlikely to lead to anything good.

As a person of experience, you can do better than that. You

can discriminate between solid reasons for a new marriage and solid reasons for continuing single. If marriage is not for you, now or ever, you need not cut yourself off from meaningful association with men in various settings of your life. On the other hand, if you have found and been found by a man who appeals to you as a potential mate, you have the best possible reason to consider marrying again. You and he can work together to build a truly vital marriage relationship.

When I was married after three and one half years of widowhood, I went across the state to share life in a busy parsonage. A number of my widow friends assumed I would never finish this book. I would "lose the viewpoint." I would forget how it felt to be a widow. I would go on to other projects, some of them predicted.

It is true that the work on the book was sidetracked for a time so that I could take full part in the life of the two churches and communities my husband served. But the interest we both felt in men and women who were widowed, as we had been, was certainly not diminished by our marriage. We empathized with each man or woman who was "left behind."

Happy as we are, John and I are both firmly convinced that if we had not found each other, our individual lives would have continued interesting and purposeful. While in the widowed state, each of us had mourned, had accepted and valued aloneness, had overcome some feelings of social isolation, and had grown as persons. Long before we had our first date, we had become a single man and a single woman, able to love someone new.

I hope that the reading of this book has helped you to realize where you are in widowhood, and has stimulated your progress into new womanhood. As you rebuild your life, surely you will extend your hand and your encouragement to others who have entered widowhood. You will be able to help them as they also change, growing from widow to woman.

NOTES

1. Gladys Kooiman, *When Death Takes a Father* (Baker Book House, 1968).

2. Mary Brite, of Omaha, Nebraska, founded an organization for widows called The Solitaires.

3. *THEOS Newsletter,* September 1975, p. 5.

4. William A. Lessa, "Death Customs and Rites," *Collier's Encyclopedia* (Crowell-Collier Press), Vol. 7, pp. 764–765.

5. Helen Hayes, quoted in Patricia O'Brien, *The Woman Alone* (Quadrangle/The New York Times Book Co., 1973), p. 234.

6. Alice Ginott, quoted by reporter Joan Titone during a Family Life Conference, *The Daily Iowan,* Feb. 13, 1976.

7. Karl Menninger and others, *The Vital Balance* (The Viking Press, Inc., 1963), p. 84.

8. Phyllis Silverman, "Widowhood and Preventive Intervention," *The Family Co-ordinator,* January 1972, p. 96.

9. Clark E. Moustakas, *Loneliness and Love* (Prentice-Hall, Inc., 1972), p. 101.

10. *Ibid.,* pp. 102–103.

11. Eda J. LeShan, *The Wonderful Crisis of Middle Age* (David McKay Company, Inc., 1973), p. 255.

12. Isabella Taves, *Women Alone* (Funk & Wagnalls Publishing Company, Inc., 1968), p. 72.

13. Jo Pullen, "Separation," appeared in the order of worship bulletin used at the service in memory of her husband, Charles Pullen, at the United Methodist Church, Ida Grove, Iowa.

14. Abigail Van Buren (Pauline Friedman Phillips), "Dear Abby," *Sioux City Journal,* Aug. 16, 1974, p. A-9. © Chicago Tribune–New

York News Syndicate, Inc., 1974. Used by permission.

15. These stages and tasks were noted by George W. Paterson in his mini-lecture "Helping the Bereaved Child," *Single Parent Family Conference Proceedings* (University of Iowa, 1976).

16. Edgar Jackson, *You and Your Grief* (Channel Press, 1961), pp. 32–33.

17. Lynn Caine, *Widow* (William Morrow & Company, Inc., 1974), pp. 202–203.

18. Sara Mast, "Moments with You," poem in memorial booklet honoring her father, Gifford Mast (Davenport, Iowa, 1972).

19. Ira O. Glick, Robert S. Weiss, and C. Murray Parkes, *The First Year of Bereavement* (John Wiley & Sons, Inc., 1974).

20. Helen Harris Perlman, *Persona* (The University of Chicago Press, 1968), p. 81.

21. Lilly Danielson Frels, "Widow Becomes a 59-Year-Old Coed to Get Her Degree," *Sioux City Journal*, Feb. 27, 1972, Associated Press.

22. Mary Halkias, "God Doesn't Make Junk!" *THEOS Newsletter*, September 1976, p. 17.

23. Sylvia Porter, *Sylvia Porter's Money Book* (Doubleday & Company, Inc., 1975), pp. 118–120. (Adapted.)

24. These steps in problem-solving are as presented by Louise C. Johnson, Associate Professor of Social Behavior, University of South Dakota.

25. Anonymous, "Through It All . . . ," *THEOS Newsletter*, March 1977, p. 19.

26. C. S. Lewis, *A Grief Observed* (The Seabury Press, Inc., 1963), p. 38.

27. Leslie F. Brandt, "The Loss of a Mate," from his *Book of Christian Prayer* (Augsburg Publishing House, 1974). Copyright 1974. Reprinted by permission of the publisher.

28. Evelyn King Mumaw, *Woman Alone* (Herald Press, 1970), p. 67 and Ch. VI.

29. *Ibid.*, pp. 68–69.

30. Alan Paton, *For You Departed* (Charles Scribner's Sons, 1969), p. 21.

31. W. C. McKain, "A New Look at Older Marriages," *The Family Co-ordinator*, Vol. 21, No. 1, January 1972, pp. 61–69.

32. Ruth Roosevelt and Jeannette Lofas, *Living in Step* (Stein & Day Publishers, 1976), p. 62.

Date Due
